Erstwild
Wales

A journey
through space & time
in the steps of
George Borrow

Nick Kingsford

"Lovely the woods, waters,

meadows, combes, vales,

all the air things wear

that build this world of Wales."

From 'In the Valley of the Elwy'
by Gerard Manly Hopkins

This book is dedicated to Bryn Caless, Cornishman, without
whose erudition, encouragement and meticulous editing it
might never have been written.

Map of North Wales

The route is shown thus

Scale 1 : 785 000

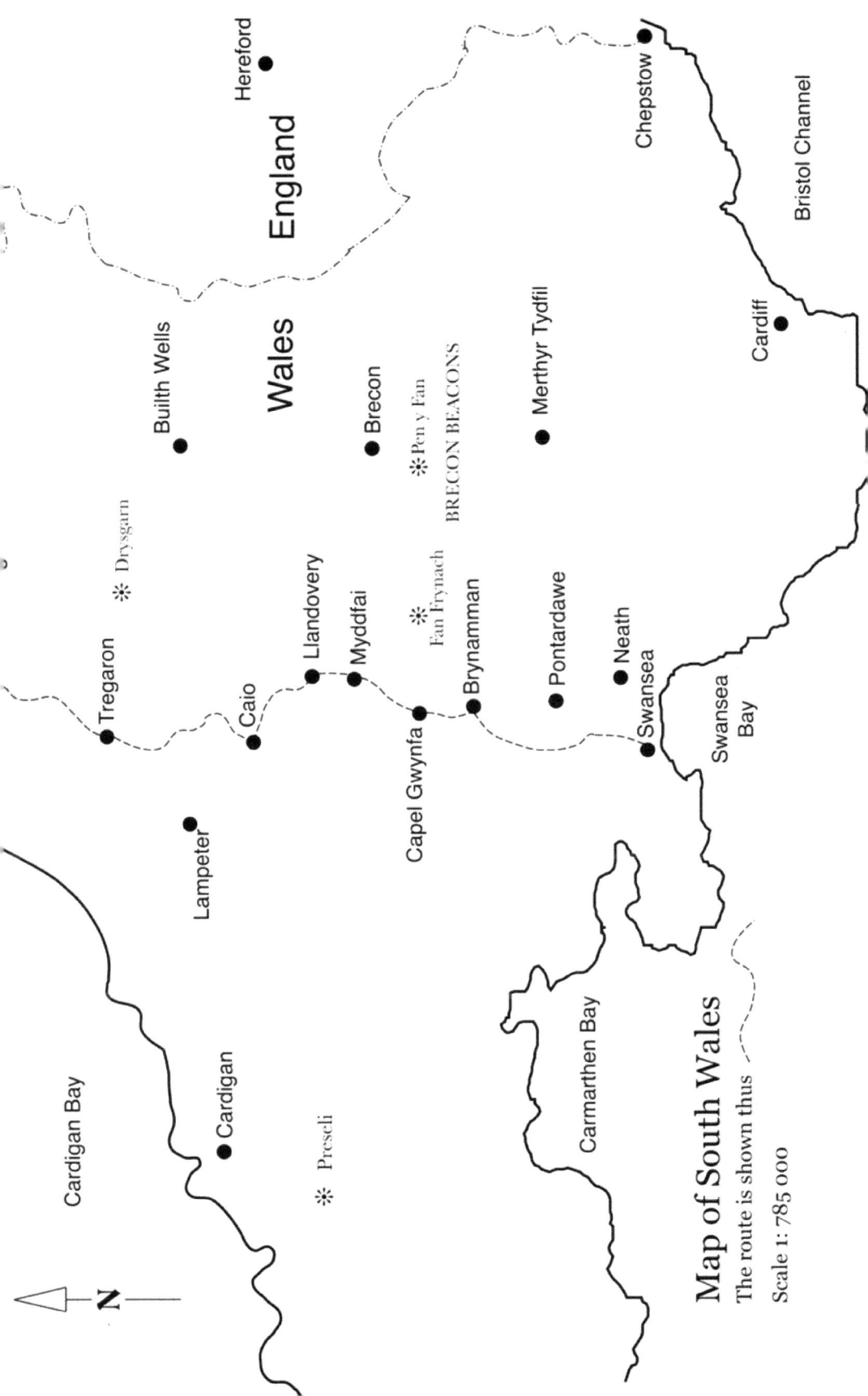

Map of South Wales

The route is shown thus ---

Scale 1: 785 000

PRE-AMBLE

In 1854 the Englishman George Borrow went walking in Wales. Nothing remarkable about that, you may think, but read on.....................

Borrow was born in 1803, the son of an army recruiting officer. He was introduced at an early age to a peripatetic life for the family accompanied Captain Borrow through England, Scotland and Ireland. By the time he was eighteen it was evident that Borrow had a huge ability with languages for he could then understand, and speak, eleven foreign tongues. He began to translate Welsh and Danish poetry into English and moved from the family home in Norwich to London in 1824. He passed several years wandering in Europe and translating ancient and modern texts into English. He was commissioned to translate the New Testament into Manchu. He spent over four years in Spain selling a Spanish version of the Bible. In 1840 Borrow married the widow Mary Clarke. He continued to travel and translate, acquiring an affinity for the gipsy people with whom he felt at home and at peace. In 1865 his wife died and five years later Borrow moved back to Norfolk. He died in Oulton on July 26 1881.

It was Borrow's knowledge of the Welsh language that motivated him to visit Wales where he hoped to put his language skills to practical use. He, his wife and their daughter Henrietta left Oulton to begin their journey, by train, to Wales on July 27 1854. At Chester, Mary and Henrietta continued by train to Llangollen but Borrow decided to walk there and arrived on August 1. Until the 27th he was content to ramble round the Llangollen district visiting ancient sites, towns, villages and enjoying the scenery. Then, wishing to see more of N. Wales, he walked to Bangor in one day. This was a prestigious feat for the distance was some 33 miles! He stayed for several days in Bangor, making day excursions, including an ascent of Snowdon, and then returned to Llangollen via Beddgelert, Llan Ffestiniog and Bala. He stayed in Llangollen with his wife and daughter until October 26 when he began his long walk to South Wales. On November 16 Borrow arrived in Chepstow where he caught a train to London.

This was a considerably adventurous expedition in the 1850s when there were no maps widely available to the public; when transport on roads was still by coach and horse; when the 'roads' were mostly muddy and stony tracks; when English travellers were still a fairly rare sight in rural Wales and when many country people spoke no English. But Borrow was a formidably strong walker, he spoke Welsh fluently, he had no difficulty in approaching and speaking to people on a wide variety of subjects and he was not daunted, as many would have been, by traversing remote moorland and lowland on foot, on his own.

Borrow kept notebooks of his daily observations and findings and used these to publish an account of his walking tour in 1862 called "Wild Wales". I first read this astonishing book in my early twenties when it fascinated and inspired me to take a further, and lifelong, interest in a country that I already knew better than most of my comtemporaries because I spent most of my weekends and holidays there, climbing rock, walking the fells and canoeing rivers.

In the early summer of 2004 "Wild Wales", by some serendipity chance, fell off my bookshelf which prompted me to delve into it anew. Whilst so doing, I realised that it was now 150 years since Borrow's walk and I conceived the idea of repeating his walk, to try to follow his route as exactly as I could, to compare the Wales of 1854 with the Wales of 2004, and to stretch my legs through some magnificent landscape, record my thoughts, observations and adventures and write them down.

Whilst "on the hoof", I had the considerable advantage of a micro-cassette recorder so I didn't have to use a pen and paper during the day. I didn't therefore have to stop to write notes, but even so I had some difficulty in maintaining Borrow's daily mileage. I consoled myself, at the end of each exhausting day, with the knowledge that I had just celebrated my sixtieth birthday whereas Borrow was only 51 at the time of his expedition. Borrow did not, of course, have such a marvel of modern technology and so it is difficult to believe that he managed to write over 500 pages about his walk without including a large quantity of fiction.

To devise a linear, fairly direct walk I decided to begin at Caernarfon, which Borrow had reached from Bangor, and follow his line to Swansea, but omitting his major detour back to Llangollen and his other diversions in central Wales. This would give a pleasing spread of landscape to cross and would be quite enough for me. I am no linguist nor do I have Borrow's erudite knowledge of obscure Welsh poets, bards and folk heroes, or of historical matters generally, and so my perceptions, comments and text would be radically different from his. Also, there can be no comparison between the way that a man perceived the world in 1854 and the way that an entirely different personality perceives the world in 2004. Borrow's background and experience were totally different from mine; he was the product of an army background and an academic adulthood whereas I was a product of art college and the swinging 60s, and of the age of the motor vehicle, computer and over-population.

I worked through "Wild Wales" comprehensively and in great detail in conjunction with the relevant OS 1:50 000 maps to determine the route he had taken and to identify the villages, inns, houses and viewpoints where he stopped for conversation, accommodation, refreshment or reflection. My choice of overnight stops differed a little from Borrow's in the middle part of the walk because he made some excursions and diversions that I didn't want to make and he spent two nights at some places, which I didn't want to do.

My broad concept was to visit all the towns, villages, houses, inns and viewpoints that I had managed to identify and to follow Borrow's general route between them. However, I'd soon realised that his line of walk, for the most part, followed exactly the line of modern main roads which are dangerous, noisy, polluted and frightening places to walk. So I decided that I would, where possible, take minor roads, tracks and footpaths so long as I could still visit the identified waypoints whilst not deviating too far from the line that Borrow had taken. This seemed a reasonable compromise.

The early routes of communication between towns and villages tended to take the line of least geographical resistance which, customarily, meant that they followed the rivers and major streams. These paths became cart tracks, then coach routes and finally the modern A-roads. Inspection of my maps showed that this was particularly prevalent in the mountainous districts of north and north-central Wales where any deviation from the valley route necessitated vast ascents and descents over the ridges and hills. In the mountainous areas, therefore, there are few quiet, walkable routes parallel with the valley routes and so I knew that I'd have to do a fair bit of road work. Furthermore, I'd have to find terrain that was easy going underfoot if I was to maintain Borrow's daily mileages or I'd be using valuable time and become exhausted by staggering around in marsh and tussock and fighting through bracken, gorse, heather and scrub.

Detailed route planning for each day was accordingly quite a difficult exercise on the map involving close inspection of the start and finish points of footpaths, judgement as to whether a detour was worthwhile to avoid road-walking and balancing the merits of height gain against detour length - the classic "over-or-round" conundrum.

In the event, there turned out to be rather too much tarmac walking, which is remarkably hard on the feet, not enough track walking and too much wading through long, wet grass. I found the public footpaths in central Wales to be appallingly badly maintained; there were broken stiles, or no stiles at all; paths impossible to reach or to follow due to excessive vegetation; there was very rarely a fingerpost showing the start of a path from a road and rarely any waymarkers showing the line of the path across fields and through woods. There were paths blocked with barbed wire or ploughed up or blocked by felled or windblown trees, and paths shown on the map that were not indicated on the ground by any means at all. I had frequently to change my route once I'd seen the condition of a path, or not even being able to find it. Access to the countryside was not a piece of cake!

My itinerary for the expedition was:

Day 1	Hereford to Caernafon	By train and bus	
Day 2	Caernarfon to Beddgelert	23km	14 miles
Day 3	Beddgelert to Llan Ffestiniog	19km	12 miles
Day 4	Llan Ffestiniog to Bala	27km	17 miles
Day 5	Bala to Minllyn	30km	19 miles
Day 6	Minllyn to Machynlleth	21km	13 miles
Day 7	Machynlleth to Ponterwyd	27km	17 miles
Day 8	Ponterwyd to Tregaron	31km	19 miles
Day 9	Tregaron to Caio	31km	19 miles
Day 10	Caio to Llandovery	14km	9 miles
Day 10	Llandovery to Brynamman	26km	16 miles
Day 11	Brynamman to Llangyfelach (N.outskirts of Swansea)	23km	14 miles
Total distance		272km	169 miles

Asterisks * in the text denote bingo points at which I was certain that I was standing in the same place as George Borrow did 150 years earlier. On some days, where his geographical narrative is sparse or where I took a different route from his to avoid main roads, there are very few of these.

***

Welsh place names can be difficult for those who have no knowledge of Welsh pronunciation or basic vocabulary. Most of the towns' names were Anglicised by the early Ordnance Survey. For example 'Llanymddyfri' became 'Llandovery'. Generally these Anglicised versions are still used. In Welsh many words mutate depending on the usage; for instance 'Bach' (small) can become 'Fach' and 'Mawr' (big) can become 'Fawr'. There has been an increase in the use of Welsh names in recent years; notably, 'Snowdonia' is now called 'Eryri' and 'The Brecon Beacons' are known as 'Bannau Brycheiniog'. I have chosen to use those names that are in most common use today.

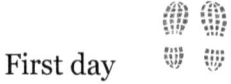

NORMANS AND KIWIS

The train journey from Hereford to Bangor was, astonishingly, without incident or delay. Whilst waiting for a bus to Caernarfon outside Bangor station I fell into conversation with an Irishman. It was slightly against my better judgement to engage down-at-heel strangers in conversation but I was determined to do as Borrow had done by speaking to anyone available. My misgivings, however, were soon realised for, without prompting, he gave me his life story in a largely incomprehensible Irish brogue. He emphatically denied that he was Irish but told me that he now lived in Australia, was in Bangor to visit his brother-in-law in Anglesey, had just come from visiting family in Ireland and was shortly to visit his family home on Merseyside. He was still talking, unstoppable and uninterruptable, when my bus arrived, ten minutes early.......or was it the previous bus ten minutes late? Anyway, I was grateful for the excuse to escape the verbal torrent. The bus was crowded, having standing room only; no-one offered this senior citizen a seat.

The sun was glowing down from a cloud-fluffed sky; the wind had been switched off for the day and the atmosphere in Caernarfon was exactly that of a mid-summer seaside town: strollers in the sunshine, ice creams in abundance, sunhats and shorts on all bodies, excited kids and a good deal of hustle and bustle. I intended to stay at The Castle Hotel*, as Borrow had done, but found that this establishment, facing the main square, no longer provided accommodation, so I paused for thought on a seat by the statue of Lloyd George. Directly before me were the massive walls and towers of the castle: an inescapable reminder of the months I had spent in Caernarfon in 1968.

Then, I'd arrived in the town in January with Frank Plowman on my first day at work as a trainee land surveyor. Frank's surveying business had been contracted by the then Ministry of Public Buildings and Works to produce a set of completely new, large-scale plans of the castle to facilitate the planning of the forthcoming investiture of the Prince of Wales. I mused on the days we'd worked in the wind and rain of a North Wales winter trying to carry out the delicate measurements needed. We'd grappled thrashing tape-measures with frigid fingers, we'd doubted the measurements taken from theodolites that vibrated in the wind, we'd struggled to write complex readings on sheets of soggy paper. I remembered cold feet, dark skies, salty spray, abseiling down the walls .... but where had we stayed?

Ah, yes! The Black Boy Inn. Now, where had it been? Somewhere near a pub called........ah, this was it: the Palace Vaults, the sight of which stirred some faint memories of smoky winter evenings with pints of M&B "brown mix". I turned into the adjacent Northgate Street and, without deviation or hesitation, I arrived at the Black Boy, a mere five minutes away. There was something subtly different about Northgate Street. A little while elapsed before I realised that it was now pedestrianised, without traffic, but with a slightly racy continental air given by one or two pavement cafes.

The Black Boy was, evidently, a little unsure as to the origin of the name for one side of the inn sign showed a black boy whereas the other showed a black buoy; perhaps in some token to the concept of political correctness. However, the date 1522 was still inscribed on the front wall and the place looked exactly as I remembered it from 1968. Enquiries within led me to the hotel reception where I mentioned to two members of the staff, both under 45, that I'd stayed there in '68 but this remark elicited no discernible interest. In due course I was allocated room 8 but it was not until I had reached the top floor and entered the room that I realised that it was the same room that I had occupied for three months all those years ago!

Having dumped my rucksac, I made my way out into the sunshine and the screaming of gulls to see how the town had changed in 35 years. Immediately I sensed a more relaxed, more colourful, quieter environment than I remembered, with a good deal more charm. It was no longer the grey, windswept, dull, rather depressed place of my memory. Many of the back streets were pedestrianised with pavement cafes, bistros and 'smart' little shops. The old streets were quiet, narrow and featured elegant period houses which I did not remember. The town seemed bright, clean and tidy, at least on that sunny summer afternoon. I suspect that the renaissance of the town had begun with the investiture of the Prince of Wales at the castle in 1969.

The castle, built by Edward 1 to secure his foothold in Wales after the death of the last Prince of Wales, did not seem to have decayed at all since my last visit but indeed struck me as being in extraordinarily good condition in view of its 900 years of existence. The massive, clean-faced, sharp-cornered stone towers and the sheer curtain walls presented an unassailable bastion of closely-fitted and hardly-weathered stone blocks. What a technical 'tour de force' to have built this in the twelfth century.

Castle Square is now an attractive paved area for pedestrians between the rows of brightly painted Georgian and Victorian houses, shops and cafes on opposite sides. There are a dozen or so mature and carefully maintained healthy London plane trees in the square which I thought had not been there in 1968. These trees surround a dominant statue of Sir Hugh Owen (1804-1881) in bronze, much larger than life-size, with long hair, but an air of considerable gravitas. The inscription was: *"...... a tireless philanthropist, he devoted his life to the establishment of non-sectarian primary schools in Wales, teacher training colleges, University of Wales and Welsh County (Intermediate) Schools".* It was odd that I should have taken note of this man, as his name was mentioned again later in the day.

In an attempt to trace Borrow's route from Caernarfon as closely as possible, I intended to find out the location of the National School at which he stopped to listen to a sermon about the harvest at a place called "Llan...something" (sic). An enquiry at the Information Centre pointed me in the direction of the Gwynedd Archives to which I duly found my way in the afternoon sunshine. This short walk showed me the northern part of the original town walls and the dock area which I did not remember at all. My enquiry, when I arrived, was whether they had any knowledge of a National School within an hour's walk of Caernarfon on the road to Beddgelert. I was conducted to the hushed cool of the main search room where all the conversation was in Welsh. I was, in short order, shown various weighty tomes, also in Welsh, featuring lists of National Schools. None of them was on the Beddgelert road. There was much discussion, in Welsh, and then my man disappeared into the bookshelves. Whilst waiting, I received a lecture from his colleague about the National Schools and their innovator who was.......none other than Sir Hugh Owen whose idea had been to introduce non-sectarian education to the area. Shortly, and to my relief, for I found that my ear was unaccustomed to the heavily accented English of the north-Walian, I was handed an aged volume which listed a National School built in 1837 at Croesywaun (The Cross in the Vale). On my map I located this as being about 3 miles from Caernarfon on the A4085 to Beddgelert. That seemed to be what I was looking for! I thanked them all with 'diolch yn fawr' and made my escape into the warmth and light of the late afternoon sunshine.

I wandered along the promenade with a view across the glittering Menai Strait to distant misty Anglesey where there were some sailing boats scudding to and fro. I paused between the old town curtain walls and the sea wall, sheltered from the wind, where the sun warmed the walls and the gulls wheeled and screeched above and remembered part of Masefield's 'Sea Fever':

> "I must go down to the seas again, for the call of the
>   running tide
> is a wild call and a clear call that may not be denied;
> and all I ask is a windy day with the white clouds flying,
> and the flung spray and the blown spume, and the sea-
>   gulls crying."
> (John Masefield 'Sea Fever')

The tourists ambled in contented groups; it was all very calm, very peaceful. My return to Castle Square involved a circumnavigation of the castle via the swing bridge and thence along the quay, for I had glimpsed what seemed to be a railway station. How odd. Surely there'd been no station here in 1968?

Well, there it was, only a stone's throw from the castle: The Welsh Highland Railway, consisting of a platform, a main track and a loop to run the locomotive to the other end of the train, and a footbridge, but no sign of any activity. My OS map did show a dismantled rail track from Caernarfon to Llanwnda where the track divided; one line going south towards Criccieth and the other swinging east across the grain of the country to Waunfawr. Beyond there, traces of the old track appeared on the map, intermittently, at Llyn Cwellyn, Beddgelert Forest, Beddgelert itself and the Aberglaslyn Pass. Could it be that new track had been laid along this route? Building new railways? How exhilarating. What a project! *(Indeed, one **can** now travel by the Welsh Highland Railway from Caernarfon to Porthmadoc)*

A leaflet I found later in the Tourist Office told me that this was an all-new railway, laid on the old track bed, funded by the Millenium Commission Lottery Fund with the eventual aim of opening the line all the way to Porthmadoc. At present the line ended at a new station at Rhyd Du which gave easy access to the Rhyd Du path up Snowdon. But a railway to Porthmadoc would connect to the Ffestiniog Railway and Blaenau Ffestiniog is served by the regular rail system, so Caernarfon would be accessible by train........a stirring possibility.

I crossed the footbridge and strolled along a terrace above the quay, where I read, on the door of a terraced house, " NO CHRONICALS PLEASE". An amusing spelling mistake. What didn't they want - people who were habitually poorly or unsolicited printed matter? I was reminded of the frequent signs on front gates when I was a teenager: **'No Hawkers or Circulars'** which I found eerily cryptic at the time.

At the Caffi Maes, in Castle Square, I stopped for a mug of tea in the sunshine. I asked the server "Are you Welsh?" She replied, " Yes, of course". I said, "Do you speak Welsh?" Again she said "Yes, of course". I then asked how many people in the town spoke the language. She said " Most people do, or at least most of the local people, the people born here or roundabouts. The incomers, the English, mostly they don't, can't be bothered, don't see any point because all us Welsh folk also speak English." It seemed that Welsh is spoken by all, except incomers and tourists, day by day, and that this had been the case as long as she could remember. My experience of eavesdropping during my brief stay in the town certainly supported this. Being amongst Welsh speakers had the peculiar effect of making me feel shut out, of being excommunicated in my own country.

Before returning to the Black Boy, I went to stand in Castle Square for a moment to wonder again at the magnificence of the castle. Whilst thus absorbed, I was accosted by a woman who asked me, in an antipodean accent, to photograph her and her husband in front of the castle. She was short, about 5'3", and rather plump; he was hugely tall (6'7" as I later found out) and thin as a rake. This indeed would be a picture of contrasts: this physically ill-matched couple in front of the venerable stonework; two Kiwis in Wales dwarfed by a Norman castle. I doubt that Borrow ever had the privilige of meeting a New Zealander.

Nearing the inn, stunned by the continual raucous screaming of the gulls, I sensed a falling object and immediately felt a wet warmth on my thigh. A quantity of gull poop had magically appeared on my leg. I later found that this was quite common, unsurprisingly, for the waitress told me that she had suffered this indignity whilst out in her best new white blouse.

I ate that evening in the inn then, after a brief stroll in search of post-prandial coffee, I retired to prepare myself for the next day's lengthy walk to Beddgelert which seemed to be unattainably distant.

***

In Welsh the single letter 'F' is pronounced 'V' so though it is spelled 'Caernarfon' it is pronounced 'Caernarvon'. The double 'F' as in Ffestiniog is, on the other hand, pronounced as an 'F' so it's not pronounced FFFestiniog but simply as 'Festiniog'.

The double 'D', as in Beddgelert, is best pronounced by making a voiced 'TH' sound as in 'there", making Beddglert sound almost as 'Bedthgelert'.

Second day

PASSING THE WOLF'S CASTLE

Breakfast at the Black Buoy was not a sociable affair as the other tables were occupied by decorators or plasterers wearing jeans covered in paint and other less salubrious solids. Their objective seemed to be to eat as much fried breakfast as they could, as quickly as possible.

To work out my route for the day I compared my OS 1:25 000 map with Borrow's text and decided that he had without doubt taken the line of what is now the A4085 but which, in his time, would have been a stony coach road. My aim was to follow this route closely but to do as little road walking as possible. I chose to follow footpaths where they ran roughly parallel with the road and not too far from it. My first way-point would be the National School at which he'd listened to a harvest sermon which, my enquiries at the Archives had shown, had most probably been at Croesywaun.

I left the inn at 8.20 on a grey, chilly morning, damp after overnight rain, to the omnipresent screeching of the gulls. Castle Square was eerily deserted after the animated, sun-drenched scene of the previous afternoon. It was threatening to rain. Beyond the outskirts of the town I crossed Pont Peblig and passed the end of the industrial sprawl where the footway at the side of the road came to an end. I now had to walk on the road itself, through typical Welsh lowland pasture country.

Ten minutes later I came to the village sign for Caeathro, where the footway resumed which pleased me somewhat as the road was fairly busy at that rush-hour time. Caeathro was an undistinguished little place whose medley of drab dwellings looked rather dreary in the grey morning. This impression was lightened slightly by the presence of a pub. The one pedestrian in sight, whom I tried to engage in conversation, rushed by with a brief "Morning". He was, evidently, not inclined to speak to rucksac-toting strangers.

Borrow wrote of departure from Caernarfon: "It might be about three o'clock in the afternoon when I left Caernarvon for Beth Gelert, distant about thirteen miles. I journeyed through a beautiful country of hill and dale, woods and meadows, the whole gilded by abundance of sunshine..........I reached a village, and asked a man the name of it. "Llan-something," he replied. As he was standing before a long building I asked him what place it was......and received for answer that it was the National School and that there was a clergyman preaching in it. The sermon was a very seasonable one, being about the harvest."

The filling station at the Caeathro roundabout was dismally deserted and beyond it the footway once again came to an end. I stepped onto the road apprehensively because road-walking, particularly A-road walking, is a dangerous and frightening procedure; drivers seem to have no understanding of the vulnerability and frailty of the human body; the majority of them make no attempt to slow down for pedestrians on the road or even to cease accelerating, and very few pull over to give a wide berth. It is this contempt for those on foot that I find so despicable. However, the traffic had by now thinned a little which reduced my fear of impending death at every approaching roar.

The sun began weakly to shine. The road led uphill past young oak and ash trees at the borders of the pastures. A little after nine I reached spot height 129, with a sigh of considerable relief, for here I could turn left and escape the trunk road with its inconsiderate drivers. There was at this point, the top of a rise in the road, a remarkable panorama of the mountains ahead comprising, as Borrow rightly remarks, Moel Eilio to the left - an elegant rounded summit - and to the right the dark, cragged, steepness of the north side of Mynydd Mawr. Between these two impressive hills was the flat vale containing the Afon Gwrfai and, higher up, Llyn Cwellyn. To the south the Nantlle ridge rose in undulating colourless silhouette against the patchy grey sky; to it's right the steel grey shimmer of the sea was a counterpoint flat plane.

I followed the by-road for 100 metres and then turned right onto a footpath through an iron kissing gate. There were shortly two more of these, all of which were too small to pass through with a rucksack on one's back. I had to negotiate them by climbing up the semi-circular fence so as to be able to swing the gate past my body. I soon found myself in a large expanse of boggy gorse and bracken where the footpath became lost in a network of sheep and horse tracks. I lost the path and its general line in this confusing maze of scrub and had to climb a fence to reach a narrow lane at Pant-y-Cerrig. A zig-zag of muddy footpaths led through scruffy smallholdings, horse paddocks, sheep enclosures and nasty little bits of marsh and waste ground to the minor road at Croesywaun which I reached at nine forty-five.

There was nothing in the immediate vicinity that could have been the National School but 400m away to the west I could see, above the trees, a substantial building in Welsh chapel style with a circular window, steep slate roof and pseudo-classical pediment which was probably the building That Borrow stopped at to listen to the sermon. However, after my recent struggle with the terrain, sweaty and brambled, I had no inclination to make a detour to verify it.

Borrow's narrative for this stretch of the route includes the following extracts: "Leaving the village of the harvest sermon I proceeded on my way which lay to the south-east. I was now drawing nigh to the mountainous district of Eryri - a noble hill called Mount Eilio appeared before me to the north; an immense mountain called Pen Drws y Coed lay over against it on the south............I entered a most beautiful sunny valley and presently came to a bridge over a pleasant stream running in the direction of the south...everything looked so beautiful or grand - green, sunny meadows lay all around me, intersected by the brook, the water of which ran with tinkling laughter over a shingly bottom........I then addressed myself to the man who had stopped, asking him the name of the bridge. "Pont Bettws," he replied".

Well, of course I had no need to ask people (even if I'd been able to find any) the names of villages and mountains for I had the Ordnance Survey's cartographic masterpieces constantly to hand. Nevertheless, I could not see that Pen Drws y Coed is visible from this far down the valley and think the hill must have been Mynydd Mawr. Mynydd Drws Coed is 3 km south of Mynydd Mawr and is not visible until one is close to Llyn Cwellyn. The bridge "over the pleasant stream" was certainly that at Betws Garmon* where the Afon Gwrfai is running north-west, not south.

I made my way, on minor roads, through Croesywaun which was a scruffy area of paddocks, rusting corrugated iron sheds and run-down cottages scattered around the fields.The slopes of Moel Eilio were now much closer and clearer, drab-green and smooth above the patches of woodland on its lower slopes. Mynydd Mawr presented a much more forbidding aspect, dark steep crags, purplish above the dense coniferous woodland called Tros y Gol'. The sun shone but briefly and intermittently through the grey overcast; there was rain in the wind but not enough to cause me to use my brolly. The umbrella, a radical and rather bizarre departure from the usual walkers kit of Goretex jacket and overtrousers would turn out later to be a very shrewd additon to my equipment.

I soon left the road by the chapel at Bryn y Pistyll and turned down a lane to a T junction where I turned left. Here the dwellings were neater and better cared-for than at Croesywaun. This settlement had more of an English village ambience where whitewashed cottages were neatly set adjacent to the lane, where red valerian sprouted from the stone walls at the lane-side and where, for the first time, I heard that hated sound: the cacophany of barking dogs.

The route followed an attractive little tarmac lane where campion, meadow sweet and ferns grew on the stone walls and where the hedges were a tangle of hazel, hawthorn, ash and flowering blackthorn. It made a refreshing and peaceful alternative to the A4085. The lane led south-east, fairly directly towards some mining waste-tips on the hillside at Treflan Isaf. I imagined that a lane so straight had been created by the quarry workers going to and from their homes at Bryn y Pistyll. Perhaps they had been better-paid than the crofters at Croesywaun and better able to care for their property. An intimate landscape of small paddocks and scattered dwellings many of which had been renovated to modern standards, implying money to spare. Some paddocks had been left for hay, now standing knee high, for a second cut perhaps; some paddocks were derelict and full of thistles, but whatever the land use the terrain was made ugly by the customary blight of corrugated asbestos farm barns, grouped in random juxtapositions across the landscape. The ground now began to rise steeply from the main road on the other side of the valley in typical ascending Welsh hill land, gappy stunted oak woodland, interspersed with small crags and sheep pasture.

By ten-fifteen I was approaching the wooded tump of Carreg Fawr through pastureland heavily populated with sheep, and their droppings. The sense of peace was heightened by the cooing of pigeons, the swooping gymnastics of swallows and the delicate hovering of flycatchers; but destroyed by those other aerial beasts - RAF jets. The path led in due course past the churchyard at Betws Garmon and onto the main road. Here, hoping to find a resident to speak to, I approached a woman waiting at the bus stop in front of the chapel. I greeted her and she returned with "Ah, a fellow wanderer. How nice." She was also a visitor, but not from far away for she lived at Aberdovey, a cyclist, touring at random as the whim took her and staying that night at the Bettws Inn which lay a short way from the bus stop. Why she was waiting for a bus I didn't ask and she didn't say.

The sight of a fine bridge just before this village made me think that this might be the Pont Bettws that Borrow referred to and that the Bettws Inn* might be the "little inn on the left side of the way at the entrance of a village" where he drank ale and questioned the resident about the name of his dog. Borrow found it bizarre that here in the depths of Welsh Wales, he should come across a dog called 'Perro' which, as a linguist, he well knew was the Spanish word for 'dog'.

Pleased as I was to have located a building at which Borrow probably stopped, I went to the Bettws Inn and knocked on the door. The proprietor, Nigel Smith, seemed interested in my project, especially when I told him that I thought that Borrow stopped for ale in 1854. He was able to offer me a potted history of the place. The Inn began as a drover's hostelry, in the mid 17th century and became a coaching inn about 1720 to serve the travellers between Cardiff and Holyhead. The inscription on the front wall of the building " M Pierce 1753" records the name of the licensee at that time when the inn was known as "The Cross Foxes". About 1810 copper mining began on the hillside behind the inn (leaving the waste tips that I'd seen earlier) which brought money into the area and required the inn to be enlarged to provide better and additional facilities. Between 1890 and the 1920s the inn was the village shop and licensed premises. Mr Smith showed me the original account book of the inn of about 1894 which recorded in great detail the daily purchases of the local people. Later the inn became a pony-trekking stable until the 1970s when it fell empty and became derelict. The present owners restored it to its present elegant and comfortable condition as a bed and breakfast establishment in 1990. I felt a frisson of historical excitement to think that I was standing where Borrow supped his ale 150 years ago. There is a slate milestone on the outside wall of the inn inscribed *"Caernarfon 5 miles. Beddgelert 8 miles."*

Half a mile later I could see a new railway line on my left which was not shown on my map but which I assumed was the Welsh Highland Railway..... would I see a train? I passed a row of terraced houses at Salem where a man from Birmingham who was replacing a window frame confirmed that the new railway line now ran as far as Rhyd Ddu; he was not a Welsh speaker. Borrow walked "rapidly on towards the east and soon drew near the termination of the valley". Borrow's sense of direction and geography are haywire here for the valley actually doesn't 'terminate' but continues to Rhyd Du and he was walking south-east.

In due course I came to the spot* where, unmistakably from his lengthy description of the place, Borrow remarks: "presently I came to a little mill by the side of the brook running towards the east. I asked the miller-woman who was standing near the mill the name of the mill and the stream". Hmm, the stream he mentions, the Gwrfai, is actually running north-west here.

There was no mill there now, on the Afon Gwrfai, but the weirs still existed as did a small water extraction works for Welsh Water. Just at this point the railway crossed the river on a brand new bridge, new track, new ballast. I was marvelling at the expense and immense amount of work that this must have incurred, when the rails began to sing. A train was on its way. Magically appearing, curving in from between the trees, an articulated, narrow-gauge steam loco, with tenders front and rear, hove into view. The unique articulation of tender-loco-tender put me to musing on the last time I saw a locomotive like that. Hmm...........must have been Nairobi railway shed in 1965. Those locos had been the famous, immensely powerful Beyer-Garratt engines used for hauling trains into and out of the East African Rift Valley. Could this, too, have been a Beyer-Garratt, albeit narrow-gauge? Well, it was too late now for the loco had passed me by. The following train of goods wagons and passenger carriages squealed and clacked through the woods, over the bridge and away up the valley. What a delight!

To avoid further road walking I had earlier intended to follow the railway track but I found that the gates across the line were locked and decided that anyway it was not very prudent to walk along a railway line when trains were running.

So I continued on the main road which was not very busy, not very wide and gave pleasant enough walking albeit hard underfoot. The slopes of Mount Eilio came right down to the road on the left. On the right, across the valley, which was narrow at this point, I could clearly see the nose of the rocky ridge falling down from Mynydd Mawr, the crag called Castell Gidwm (Wolf's

18

Castle) to which Borrow refers. The valley was a mere 300 metres wide but still cluttered with knolls, boulders, small crags, rocky tumps and patches of woodland.

As I rounded the bend in the road at Tyn Weirglodd the vast, placid, gleaming sheet of Llyn Cwellyn* came into sight, filling the valley so that the hillsides on either side slid straight into the sheet of gunmetal grey. Just here Borrow commented: "I at last emerged from the pass into a valley surrounded by enormous mountains. Extending along it from east to west, and occupying its entire southern part lay an oblong piece of water into which the streamlet of the pass discharged itself". Borrow's sense of up and down was faulty too for the River Gwrfai runs out of Llyn Cwellyn and not into it.

The map showed a path through the forest, parallel with the lake shore, on the other side of the lake and I hoped to be able to cross the outfall stream at the lake's north-western end to reach it. There the map showed two close parallel lines that might imply a footbridge. At all events, I would investigate. The property occupying the land at the end of the lake seemed to be a holiday establishment of some sort with a single storey, bungalow-style main block and sundry outhouses, cottages and caravans. It was deserted and no-one answered my knock on the door nor was there anyone in evidence.The property had no name but there was a large 'PRIVATE' sign on the front gate. I walked through the gardens along the lakeside to the outfall stream and discovered a weir but no means of crossing the wide watercourse which was running strongly. Even if there had been, there were two signs on the opposite bank which displayed 'Cwm Bychan private', so the right of way shown on the map along the lake shore was unattainable. I returned to the road and continued along the lakeside. I mused that I had met only 3 people this morning to talk to, plus the road repair team who were working at the site of the former mill, one of whom waved the traffic through a red traffic light, so I said to him " It's hard for a driver to drive through a red light", to which he replied "Yes, indeed, isn't it?".

Foxgloves, campion and cow's parsley and ash, willow, brambles and oak populated the narrow strip of land betweent the road and the lake shore. Clear felling had been carried out in the forest across the lake leaving the usual ugly, brown, scarred, bare mess on the hillside. As I progressed along the lakeside the lower slopes of Moel Eilio dropped back from the lakeside to leave room for pasture land dotted with farm buildings. The narrow-guage railway was now visible, on my left, following the line of the former railway, shown as 'dismantled railway' on the map. It had, I recollected, crossed under the road just at the end of the lake so my idea of walking down the railway to reach the path across the lake would not have been feasible.

Borrow then " wandered a considerable way without meeting or seeing a single human being". Well, that hadn't changed in 150 years, for nor did I. Soon he "saw two men in the vicinity of a house which stood a little way up the hill". This house I believe is still there and now called Llwyn Onn. He commented that " the lake here was much wider than I had hitherto seen it for the huge mountain on the south had terminated." This was an optical illusion as Llyn Cwellyn is pretty much the same width along its length. And mountains really don't 'terminate', do they?

His conversation with the two men was a lengthy exchange. He asked: "What is the name of the great black mountain there on the other side?". The reply was: " It is called Mynydd Mawr or the Great Mountain. Yonder rock which bulks out from it, down the lake yonder, is called Castell Cidwm, which means Wolf's Castle." The modern map still gives this name for that rocky buttress.

Borrow enquired of the younger man: "What profession does your father-in-law follow? Is he a fisherman?". "Fisherman!" said the elderly man contemptuously, "not I, I am the Snowdon Ranger." (This contempt for fishermen is interesting for I recall that, as late as the early nineties, when frightened or stuck on a rock-climb one would traditionally exclaim: "To hell with this, I'm taking up fishing!).

Their conversation continued: " And what is that?" I asked. "A ranger means a guide, sir," said the younger man, " gentlemen put themselves under his guidance to ascend Snowdon." Borrow had already found out that the younger man was a miner, so he wittily remarked: "There is some difference in your professions, he deals in heights, you in depths, both, however, are break-necky trades."

I, however, met no-one with whom to exchange repartee, not even when I approached the Snowdon Ranger Youth Hostel which is immediately at the roadside. At least the origin of the name of the Youth Hostel is now apparent even though it is not the house where the Ranger lived, at least not in 1854. The patch of woodland between the road and the lake is now used to park cars. The Snowdon Ranger path to the summit of Snowdon led up the hillside just before the hostel, marked, curiously enough, as a bridleway. I don't imagine than many people aspiring to reach the top of Wales' highest summit would be climbing on horseback!

Ten minutes beyond the hostel I could see the end of the lake. Mynydd Mawr had become merely a ridge on the other side. But beyond and to its left was a fine, pyramidical peak faced almost entirely with rock which I considered was the east side of Mynydd Drws y Coed. A little further on, the train I'd seen earlier rumbled into sight going in the opposite direction, back towards Caernarfon. And what an incongruous sight it was; the articulated loco towing a train through the rather bare Welsh upland countryside where normally one would see stone walls, upland pasture and sheep. One expected to see the usual spare mountainside but there was this panting, whistling, noisy, mechanical snake pouring smoke, steam and noise into the landscape. It looked bizarrre, and out of place, but a pleasure to see, none the less, and reassuring to know that someone had considered the enormous investment in this new railway to be worthwhile.

Borrow enjoyed the view of the lake and the narrowing valley at the far end from this point for he wrote: "I sped along......after a time I looked back; what a scene! The silver lake and the shadowy mountain over its southern side looking now, me-thought, very much like Gibraltar". (*Gibraltar, for goodness' sake, had his power of perception deserted him?)* It looked nothing like that barren rock for indeed the backward view was a very satisfying blend of lake, hill, woodland and rock; and now that the sky had large patches of blue the lake had changed colour from steel grey to steel blue. I was now a mere kilometre from Rhyd Ddu, where I knew there was a pub, so I was keenly anticipating a pint or two with my bread and ham.

There was quite a steep ascent into the village of Rhyd Ddu* but the Cwellyn Arms soon came into sight. My thirst was so great that I ordered two pints together. The publican was evidently not very pleased when I asked if I could eat my bread and ham whilst drinking the beer I had bought from him. He reluctantly agreed but said, "Don't be too obvious about it. If everyone did that, we'd be out of business". So I hid away in the 'beer garden' which was a paved back yard containing rubbish bins and empty beer kegs. I enjoyed my ale, which in all truth, went down without touching the sides, whilst pondering my route for the afternoon. I'd had enough road walking for one day and so I chose a footpath route round the west side of Llyn y Gâder and into Beddgelert Forest. This path was not defined on the ground at all to the west of the lake nor was it signposted. Consequently, when I met the edge of the forest I was not sure where I was on that line so I struggled south-west hoping to find the forest corner. My body was fully engaged in this toil but my mind was not and it found some lines from 'The Way through the Woods' by Kipling:

> "They shut the way through the wood
>   seventy years ago.
> Weather and rain have undone it again,
>   and now you would never know
> there was once a road through the woods
>   before they planted the trees."

The forest corner was not as clearly defined as the map suggested but, after using my compass for a while, I eventually found the forest road and duly arrived back at the main road at Pont Cae'r Gors*. Borrow "reached a torrent, which coming from the north-west rushed under a bridge, over which I passed". This was doubtless Pont Cae'r Gors, but the Afon Colwyn is flowing from the north-east.

From there I followed forestry tracks and paths, determined to avoid the main road through the forest and patches of open land within it. By three thirty I had crossed a bridge over the Afon Meillionen and stopped for a rest in the corner of a meadow at the woodland edge. The path I tried to follow through Parc Ty'n y Coed was abundantly overgrown with an appalling tangle of windblown trees, brambles, stinging nettles, young scrub and bracken but I found an alternative, fairly well-used path through bog and marsh and eventually came to the farm at Cwm Cloch Isaf.

Nearing Beddgelert, Borrow commented: "I found myself amongst houses, at the bottom of a valley. I passed over a bridge and inquiring of some people whom I met, the way to the inn, was shown an edifice brilliantly lighted up which I entered". He doesn't mention the name of the inn, which could have been any one of several in the village.

For me, the route from the farm into Beddgelert was straightforward and I arrived at the Tourist Office at quarter past four. The Old Goat Inn was closed 'for maintenance' so I asked at the Office if they could find me a room for the night. I was duly booked in at the Bryn Eglwys Hotel and given directions as to how to get there.

Beddgelert, a popular tourist centre, is very trim and tidy, almost immaculate, situated on a clear, shallow, river confluence; neat, painted cottages enclosed the green; a fine stone bridge spanned the river; shops and cafes clustered together in the beautiful setting deep in the hills; Moel Hebog towered over the village. The hotel was very well appointed, very comfortable and very welcoming but the restaurant was expensive so I dined in the village. En route to my supper I stopped at the village shop to re-acquaint myself with the proprietor who I'd known in 1972 when he was a close neighbour in Hertfordshire; we had trouble in recognising each other.

Borrow's description, in chapter 46, of Beddgelert is: "Beth Gelert is situated in a valley surrounded by huge hills, the most remarkable of which are Moel Hebog and Cerrig Llan; the former fences it in on the south, and the latter, which is quite black and nearly perpendicular, on the east. A small stream rushes through the valley and sallies forth by a pass at its south-eastern end."

Beddgelert means 'The Grave of Gelert'. The legend is a moving one though doubtless fictitious. Gelert was the faithful dog of one Llywelyn ap Jowerth, a Welsh warrior battling with the English, who left his camp one day leaving his baby son in the tent in the care of his trusty hound. During Llywelyn's absence a wolf came down from the hills smelled fresh baby and entered the tent. Gelert intercepted the beast and a bloody fight ensued which collapsed the tent and in which the wolf was finally destroyed. When Llywelyn returned he found a collapsed tent and his blood-smeared dog sitting beside it. Thinking, as one would, that the dog had killed his baby son, Llywelyn in a rage, killed Gelert with his spear. Immediately he heard a cry from under the collapsed tent and, removing the blood-stained canvas, found his son in his cradle, quite un-harmed, next to the mangled body of a huge wolf. Gelert had saved his son from the wolf but Llywelyn had mis-read the scene and slayed his faithful dog. Llywelyn mourned the dog, buried him with a proper funeral and erected a tomb fit for a hero. Hence the name Beddglert.

***

The sound of the frequent 'LL' as in Llandudno, is best made by putting the tonue behind the top teeth (as one would to sound an 'L') and holding it there whilst breathing out through the sides of the mouth. It is not a 'CL' sound nor 'FL', so it's **not** 'Clandudno' or 'Flandudno' as I have so often heard it mutilated.

The former inn at Bettws where Borrow stopped

Llyn Cwellyn

The Aberglaslyn Gorge showing the old railway embankment and tunnel

Cnicht

STONECHATS AND TRAMWAYS

I left Beddgelert just before nine o'clock on a dull, cool morning by means of a concrete path along the riverside through well-manicured parkland in the direction of Aberglaslyn. The river on my right was shallow, fast flowing and crystal clear; the air was damp with impending rain. Ten minutes later I passed a footbridge over the river where the path became the dismantled railway of the former line from Caernarfon to Porthmadoc presumably. Underfoot now was a stony track leading into narrower terrain where the hillsides came down to the river, which became noisier and busier, showing more white water amongst the boulders. There were interlocking spurs ahead suggesting bends in the river. The low hillsides on either side were studded with rock scree, bracken, mountain ash and scrub. Shortly the path was diverted to the right to avoid walking through the tunnels of the old railway which, a sign informed me, had been declared dangerous. This old fishermen's path rapidly became a rocky scramble with some quite difficult moves for a 60 year old carrying 14kgs. It weaved its way, very close to the water, over rocky spurs, slippery boulders and little pebbly beaches. Twenty metres above, a finely built stone retaining wall contained the dismantled railway against the cliff.

Borrow describes the view "at the entrance to the pass" of Aberglaslyn and goes on to say: "Truly the valley of Gelert is a wondrous valley - rivalling for grandeur and beauty any vale either in the Alps of Pyrenees." Well, I would take issue with this and though the valley to the south of Beddgelert is very charming and peaceful it by no means compares with the Fier valley in the Haute Savoie or the Cirque de Gavarnie in the Pyrenees. Oddly he doesn't mention the gorge of the pass of Aberglaslyn itself which is the most impressive feature hereabouts.

I enjoyed the rough path, scrambling over boulders, and down slippery slabs in the middle of the Aberglaslyn gorge. White water crashed over the boulders and down the rapids; the heavy, luxuriant greenery sagged over the rushing torrent. It was a savage, wild canyon, apparently unspoilt by the hand of man because the A498 was on the other bank, hidden in the vegetation and inaudible for the traffic roar was drowned by the seething water. I had driven that road many times since my teens but I'd never walked on this side where one could truly experience the wild situation at first hand rather than being insulated from it by the cabin of a car.

"But, O, that deep romantic chasm which slanted
down the green hill athwart a cedarn cover!
A savage place!"
(From Coleridge's Kubla Khan)

In what seemed like no time at all, the bridge* at Aberglaslyn came into sight with its well-remembered stone house at the road side. It was obviously the same bridge that Borrow commented on at this spot. I paused for a drink and watched a pair of cormorants, startled by my presence, flapping their wings and then slowly taking off and flying fast and directly downstream, and away from the human threat. I followed a short path through the rise and fall of the oak woodland, where boulders and crags glistened moistly, to a car-park where I joined the main road for a few yards before turning off up the lane to Nantmor.

The line of the old railway was discernible here just before the village, a pretty place whose stone cottages were scattered along the road, shrouded in garden flowers and encompassed with rhododendron bushes, oak, ash and alder. The Calvinist chapel at Nantmor was built in 1868, later than Borrow's visit. He doesn't mention a village shortly after Aberglaslyn and so it is by no means certain that he passed through Nantmor but examination of his route makes it quite likely.

I hadn't seen anyone so far, not a soul except a man who came out of a house in the village, talking to his mobile phone whilst getting into his car - a small cameo of how we live now. I'd passed through Nantmor by half past nine leaving the big mountains behind and returning to the land of well-cropped sheep pasture, undulating stands of oak and ash, rocky hillocks and little crags.

The landscape was all very green, moist and fertile. The summit of Moel Hebog was still visible over my shoulder, cloud-shrouded and forbiddingly grey. Directly ahead, the triangular wedge of Cnicht*, sharp and steep, unburdened by cloud, rose into the turgid sky.

Hereabouts, Borrow "stopped again to admire the scenery. To the west was the Wyddfa (Snowdon); full north was a stupendous range of rocks; behind them a conical peak seemingly rivalling the Wyddfa itself in altitude; between the rocks and the road where I stood was beautiful forest scenery......the wonderful conical hill impaling heaven; confronting it to the south-east was a huge lumpish hill" He asked a local resident, a tenant of a certain Mr Blicklin, the name of the "wonderful conical hill" and was told that it was Cnicht. The lumpish hill, he was informed, was known as The Great Hill which I could identify as Moelwyn Mawr.

I covered the switchback of the road at my customary speed of five kilometres an hour. On the last rise the view magically expanded to include flat river valley meadows to the right, as Borrow mentions after speaking to Mr Blicklin's tenant.

The farm shown on the map as 'The Farmyard' was one no longer for it was forlornly derelict and abandoned. I saw no sign of Borrow's crag "exceedingly lofty and of very frightful appearance". Just before ten o'clock I came to Bwlchgwernog, which I took to be his "small neat cottage at the turn of the road". It was a turn no longer, but a T junction and the cottage was deserted. Not derelict for there were signs of recent woodcutting by the side gate, but there was no-one at home in the single-storey house nor about the rather neglected site. So I certainly was not offered tea, as he was, much to his disgust, for he wanted ale.

Borrow asked his hostess if the sea had ever come up to there and surmised, himself, that it had done so. This was good thinking by Borrow because in the early 1800s the Cob causeway was built at Porthmadoc, over which the narrow-guage railway and the A497 now run, thus shutting off the whole of the Afon

Glaslyn floodplain from the sea and releasing the land for agriculture. Borrow evidently didn't know this. Prior to that, the sea used to reach Aberglaslyn, hence the name meaning "The mouth of the Glaslyn"

On his departure Borrow was directed to a "by-road behind the house which led over the hill" rather than following the "broad" road. I thought I could see this probable route on the map and so followed a track which led southerly from the T junction and soon swung to run northeast. Within a hundred metres or so, the track ended at a gate in a stone wall. Beyond, a wide grassy path led up and across the undulating hillside, through rampant bracken speckled with gorse bushes. It had been a well-made track for the original bed-stones were still visible between the grasses and, I suspected, it had been a drover's road across the hills to provide a short cut to the village of Croesor, which was my next destination. I was interested to read that Borrow got lost hereabouts and "wandered about for nearly two hours amidst rocks, thickets and precipices". He also wrote:" I was scorched by the sun, which was insufferably hot *(huh, not for me it wasn't)* and my feet were bleeding from the sharp points of the rocks which cut through my boots like razors." (Surely a gross exaggeration?) Oddly, he introduced a Welsh word into his text here, without explanation or translation, the word "anialwch". Anyway, he seemed to have had a hard time of it, though I imagine that the drover's road must have existed at that time. Borrow didn't report many other instances of losing his way and he never mentions the use of a compass, which, in view of his lack of maps, might have been a wise navigational aid. I'd already found mine useful.

Shortly after ten o'clock I stopped for a breather at the south end of Carreg Bengam where the track passed through a stone wall at the end of this crusty little ridge. Stonechats whistled and clacked at me from the bracken tops; a pair of ravens wheeled and somersaulted overhead, croaking their presence. Cnicht had now disappeared behind the lower slopes of Yr Arddu. Its place, as the dominant hill in the view of the moment, had been taken by the huge rounded summit of Moelwyn Mawr which rose directly ahead against the grey and windy sky, but was obscured momentarily by a brief rain shower. I crossed a stream and climbed the slope beyond to the ridge where the path levelled off to give a fine view of the imposing triangle of Cnicht's south face from which the gusting wind was blowing tattered rags of grey cloud. Away to the south the Nantlle ridge was etched sharply, dark against the rainclouds. The sea was still just visible from this elevated view point as a steel-grey glimmer.

I walked on the level for several minutes and then the track descended down a gully where the sun was dappling the mossy boulders. Stunted oak and ash trees grew amongst tall grasses with seeding heads in this fertile little valley. The track became a road; I topped a rise and there before me lay the village of Croesor. The chapel, at the village edge, was dated 1865, built ten years after Borrow was here but, interestingly, the first sounds I heard in the village were the voices of three elderly folk tending the churchyard and speaking Welsh. A little further on, by the bridge over the river, there was a party of schoolchildren listening to their teacher telling them about Croesor's famous water turbine. I joined the circle of youngsters to listen as well.

The turbine had been built just upstream from the village in the 1870s to create electricity for the neighbourhood, which was one of the first in Wales to have an electricity supply. He drew a comparison between the tiny local generator, which is still producing electricity for the village, and the massive, modern, pumped-storage scheme at Llanberis. The valley is very lush, well-wooded, not deep or wild, but comforting in its rural tranquillity, the softness of which is sharply emphasised by the towering wedge of Cnicht which dominates the vale. Borrow doesn't mention Croesor at all which is rather surprising in view of its beauty. He must have crossed the valley even if he didn't visit the village itself.

I continued straight on, over a crossroads and shortly paused to enjoy the spectacular view down the valley to Porthmadoc, the wide expanse of the sandy river estuary at low tide, and the distinctive double-topped hill behind Porthmadoc. The vale of green meadows studded with high-summer trees was unnaturally flat in this region of hill and dale, a flatness that accentuated the rugged hillsides above and diminished the stretch of dark golden sand at the edge of the grey smear of the sea.

I followed a fine little Welsh inland country road, three metres wide, deserted, quiet and gated, leading from Croesor to Tan y Bwlch. The tarmac wound steeply up and down, crossing the ridges and valleys to its high point at 259 metres where it cut through a strip of coniferous forest. At the spot height I stopped for a drink and a rest, but not for long because the midges soon found me in that damp, airless, marshy place blanketed by rebarbative Sitka spruce trees. At the far edge of this impenetrable greenery I was recompensed for my midge bites by a truly astonishing view of the whole of Traeth Bach, Penrhyndeudraeth, Porthmadoc, the convoluted coastline of the estuary, the pancake-flat rabbit warren of Morfa Harlech, the narrow bar at Harlech Point, and the sea of Tremadoc Bay enclosed by the distant and misty hills of the Lleyn Peninsula. A view like this, of this particularly elegant and varied terrain, is impossible to see from the main roads hereabouts as they tend to stay on the low, flat land and so it is a special reward for those who make the effort to move inland, uphill and on foot.

As I was musing on the impoverished lives of those who never walk anywhere, whilst deriving huge pleasure from the sublime view, I heard the sound of a car. A BMW sports car hurtled into view and squealed to a stop at the gate closed across the road. Both young occupants eyed the gate malevolently. "Surely we're not going to have to get out to open a gate", they seemed to be thinking. Well, no, they didn't have to because I opened it for them then, with a call of "no problem", they roared through and away through the trees - without a glance at the view that was so entrancing. Impoverished lives indeed!

I walked on towards the rolling hills and pinewoods far off in the grey distance and glimpsed the cooling towers of Trawsfynydd Power Station directly ahead; a cruel reminder of a more hostile and frightening environment. I thought briefly of Chernobyl. At eleven fifteen I passed the cottage of Ogof Llechwyn on a rise between two stream valleys and began a steep descent towards the forest to the west of Tan y Bwlch. Modern technology had found its way to this remote spot for the next stream featured a small water-treatment plant where a solar panel stood in fine testimony to common sense by not despoiling the environment further with more overhead electricity cables. It was certainly the cheaper method of supplying power to this remote treatment works. This was the second of these solar-powered water-treatment plants I had seen on this route.

The road entered another pine forest. At a bend I took a footpath on the left which led me in no time to a footbridge over the Ffestiniog Railway line and onto the platform of Tan y Bwlch *station. There were no trains in view but plenty of trippers cluttered the tea room terrace with push chairs, dogs, kids and mobile phones, trampling uneaten cake and soggy sandwiches underfoot. I unshouldered my pack and went to buy some coffee.

The railway was opened in 1832 to enable horse-drawn trams to pull empty wagons from the seaport at Porthmadoc to Blaenau Ffestiniog where they were loaded with slate from the Llechwedd Slate Mine. The wagons then returned to Porthmadoc under the force of gravity so the track had had to be laid to a consistent gradient to prevent the unpowered wagons from coming to a halt on a level stretch. Steam locos didn't start hauling wagons until the 1870s. In 1954 restoration of the now decrepit railway began. For two decades the track ended at Dduallt until a way was found to continue the line past the Tan y Grisiau reservoir, the construction of which had put the original trackbed under deep water. The line, therefore, was here in Borrow's time and it's strange that he doesn't mention it for he must have crossed it at some point and it is a very notable industrial feature in a predominantly rural region.

After a rest of half an hour I joined the B4410 and strolled past the placid waters of the lovely little Llyn Mair. The lake was fringed with oak woodland whose even canopy was broken here and there by the spire-tops of spruce and fir. I heard the whistle and exhaust chuff-chuff of a train in the trees across the lake and was sad not to see it; the woodland there was pretty dense. I passed several little lay-bys cut into the hillside at the edge of the road, in one of which a friend and I had slept in the summer of 1962. Bill had tried, without success, to catch our breakfast in the lake. Pertinently there was a group of gulls on the lake, suggesting that the fish he was unable to catch were indeed resident in the lake. I tried to remember if there is a collective noun for sea-gulls; perhaps "a screech of gulls"?. It was such an idyllic scene with very little traffic on the road. I imagined it hadn't changed much since the 1850s and I was again surprised that Borrow didn't mention the idyllic Llyn Mair.

However, a few minutes later it became apparent that perhaps this beauty spot had not existed when he walked by, for there was a small dam in the river bed at the lake's outflow point indicating that the lake had been man-made, and probably in the last 150 years.

At 12.30 I reached the Oakley Arms Hotel on the main road at Tan y Bwlch. There was no sign of any other hostelry. I was expecting to find The Grapes Inn, where Borrow "called for brandy and water", for that was where he stopped, at what he was told was Tan y Bwlch. However, examination of his text suggests that the inn he visited was in Maentwrog (whose name he doesn't mention) , because he refers to a "town" which Tan y Bwlch certainly is not, and because he found on leaving the inn that he had come past the road to Ffestiniog and had to go back.

The bar of the Oakley Arms was welcoming enough with a real fire burning in the grate and a choice of real ales but the TV was on, so I took my beer outside into the damp and rather chilly day. The terrain near the hotel was densely wooded with ornamental trees, copper beech, oak and ash and exotic conifers suggesting a planted parkland rather than naturally seeded growth. The fabric of the hotel was unusual in that it appeared to be constructed of dovetailed railway sleepers. On closer inspection I found that these large blocks were in fact slate blocks laid with thin mortar courses and elegantly mitred at the corners of the bay windows. It was over 400 years old, I had been told by the barmaid.

I finished my beer, sitting on the huge slate slabs at the front entrance, and then took the minor road on the north side of the flat Vale of Maentwrog.

Between Tan y Bwlch and Llan Ffestiniog Borrow's narrative is concerned entirely with his musing on the celebrated bard, Rhys Goch of Eryri, and with the conversation he had with an "old fellow" with a " crusty and rather conceited look", whereas I, with no such distractions, could enjoy my surroundings.

The A496 on the other side of the vale was hidden in the trees and far enough away to be inaudible. A recent floodbank or bund, on my side of the river, obscured the river itself. Between my road and the bund were sheep pastures, very full of sheep.The ground rose steeply to my left, where there were scattered copses of woodland showing a great variety of height and species and colour. Pasture land sloped upwards, its steepness increasing with altitude, to the mountain wall where tended land abruptly ended and the wild hillside began. There were signs of agricultural activity for I passed some sheep pens where sheep dogs and dozens of sheep were milling about in an apparent noisy confusion of dog bark and sheep baa. A solitary farmer was spraying sheep bottoms to remove nasty ovine worms. It was all very pastoral and clean and tidy.

This perception was rudely shattered as I progressed towards Pont Talybont. I came to a dilapidated farm on the right of the road, not defunct evidently, but in an incredible mess. The buildings were ramshackle, the farm yards and surrounds were made foul by piles of rotting black plastic, mounds of coloured plastic bins and tubs, rusting forlorn machinery, broken gates, collapsed fences, trails of coloured bailer twine trodden into the mud, sheets of disintegrating corrugated iron flapping in the breeze, split bags of fertiliser spilling their obnoxious contents onto the road verge, rotting tree limbs and fence posts, decayed wire fencing, tumbled-down stone walls. The riverside meadows were littered with sheep wool and the road with sheep dung. The rural idyll had been destroyed at a stroke.

"Ill fares the land, to hastening ills a prey,
where wealth accumulates, and men decay."
(from Oliver Goldsmith's 'Sweet Auburn')

At the end of this agricultural nightmare the lane looped over the river by an elegant, four-arched bridge built of the local schisty slate. The pointed cutwaters between the arches were extended, in classic "packhorse bridge" style above the roadway where the triangular recesses used to serve as passing places. I enjoyed the ancient structure, notwithstanding the filthy and polluted land behind me. A short steep ascent led me to the main road where, in complete contrast to the dirt and neglect behind the bridge, the owner of the house at the junction had erected some tidy trellis fencing with an arched top, neatly creosoted but looking rather urban against the rural backdrop. The road here at Pont Talybont was a roaring, fume-filled gully, across which I scooted smartly and entered the woods immediately opposite.

A footpath led steeply up the hill, through the pleasant, natural deciduous woodland following the line of the Afon Cynfa. Soon I was out on the steep open hillside where bracken was encroaching on the sheep-grazed turf. I stopped to sit in the incipient drizzle to enjoy the view down the Vale of Maentwrog which was yet more extensive now. Borrow admitted that he didn't know the name of this vale but named it the Valley of the Numerous Streams. Moelwyn Bach bulked huge across the vale, its hillside features dimmed by the drizzle-murk but the reservoir dam wall was just visible below the greyness of the flat cloud base.

It was now merely a short step to Ffestiniog which I reached just after two o'clock. It was just as well, for the drizzle was now thickening into proper rain. Searching for accommodation in the small town I came to the Abbey Arms whose ground-floor windows were boarded over. The glass in the first-floor windows was smashed - so I wouldn't be staying there!

I found a room at the Pengwern Arms, with some reluctance, as the place looked rather neglected and generally in need of a lick of paint and a good scrub. There was litter blowing about in front of the main entrance and into the foyer. Borrow described the hotel as "a large, old-fashioned house standing near the church; the mistress of it was a queer-looking old woman, antiquated in her dress and rather blunt in her manner." Next to the hotel was the rather grim-looking, slate-block built St Michaels Church in Wales, in austere Welsh style with a small belfry and surrounded by grey gravestones; it was all rather joyless. The gates to the churchyard were locked so I couldn't get in but by peering through the railing I glimpsed a headstone dated 1831. All the inscriptions were in Welsh.

An information board by the churchyard wall announced the following facts for the curious visitor: *"Most of the stone-built houses in Llan Ffestiniog are Victorian but many are far older, and parts of Pengwern Arms date from 1728. The church was built in 1845 to replace an earlier place of worship on the same site. Some gravestones bear inscriptions from the early 18th C. The village was formerly an important stop-over for drovers as they travelled to the cattle markets in England."* A knoll, to the west of the church, boasted some damp and mossy seats and was evidently the local viewpoint. From it I could see the towers of Trawsfynydd power station rising above the hills, beyond which miles of fine, green, wooded undulating countryside stretched away to the vague and grey horizon. The rain began to vent its considerable fury on my skimpy umbrella bringing with it a sudden chill so I didn't linger too long in that rather cheerless spot.

The remainder of the village had little to recommend it. Borrow wrote; "It was small and presented nothing very remarkable." As for me, I was depressed by the drab and unattractive houses and the grey and colourless environment. I visited the one village shop that was open and heard Welsh being spoken by the proprietors and their customers. Unusually, bananas were individually priced at 25p. There was one other shop and a post office, both of which were closed on a Thursday afternoon.

The Pengwern Arms was old-fashioned inside, gloomy and faintly redolent of cooking fat, tobacco smoke and another reek........perhaps of old carpets and dusty furniture. Borrow depicted the parlour as "large and rather dreary". However, the sombre atmosphere was relieved by the framed potted history of the inn hanging on the wall in the foyer which acknowledged that Borrow stayed there in 1854 and gave this description of the place:-

"The Pengwern Arms is a traditional coaching inn, listed by CADW, and dates back to the fourteenth century. It was at one time the smithy for the Pengwern Estate whose arms appear in the adjoining churchyard. In the eighteenth century there were three taverns here and this one was occupied by David Owen whose daughter Martha became famous as an inn-keeper and the pub was called Ty Martha" (Martha's House)

I heard Welsh spoken in the bar but most locals use an eclectic mix of both English and Welsh. Conversation, as far as I could tell, centered around football, mobile phones and TV. The youngsters of the town, in the absence of anywhere else to hang out, used the hotel lobby as a meeting place and so there was much raucous shouting and cackling at the entrance of the hotel. I did, nevertheless, partake of an excellent meal: two courses and a pint for under £8. (That was in 2004!)

***

The letter 'U' is pronounced in Welsh as a short 'i' as in 'dig'. Thus it sounds as 'Llandidno' not 'Llandudno'.

The letter 'O' is a short sound as in 'dog'.

The very common ocurrence of the letter 'W' can make words unintelligible for non-Welsh speakers but it is simply an "oo" sound as in 'book' (depending, as so much pronunciation does, on your own regional accent).

The two letters together 'CH' in Welsh is a guttural sound made in the back of the throat as in the Scottish word 'loch'.

Fourth day

FREE TEA AND ATTEMPTED HOMICIDE

At breakfast, where I was offered the usual indigestible, gut-filling fry-up, I shared the meal with Scots, Geordies and English. But what they were doing in such a moribund corner of Wales, I didn't find out for, at breakfast, conversation was evidently not required.

I left the Pengwern Arms before eight-thirty, glad to leave the dismal town, under an overcast sky of lowering cloud replete with the scratching cries of jackdaws. Schoolkids were kicking the kerbs while waiting for their bus outside the new bungalows and renovated houses on the outskirts. The skyline of the Moelwyns to my left was a hard-etched switchback against the silver nimbus. Borrow commented: "A mighty mountain rises in the north almost abreast of Ffestiniog; another towards the east divided into two of unequal size." The mighty mountain was doubltess Moelwyn Mawr, which is in fact north-west of Llan Ffestiniog. The other two, which he was informed were called Mynydd Mawr and Mynydd Bach, to the east, could only have been Arenig Fawr and Arenig Fach. On the other hand, knowing of Borrow's rather imprecise sense of the points of the compass, they could have been Manod Mawr and Manod Bach but these are to the north.

The unrelenting gradient led me past boundary walls made from slate blocks laid flat on each other and fences of slate slabs standing on end, pushed into the ground and loosely joined by rusty wire, silhouetted like sarsen stones against the sky.

It was a dire toil, struggling uphill early in the day on a road rising up into moorland country. In a short while I could see the gigantic piles of slate waste that are the dominating feature of the other Ffestiniog - Blaenau Ffestiniog - where rows of light coloured houses stood out sharply against the grey mountains of shale and mining detritus. I passed the entrance to Llan Ffestiniog golf club, an improbable recreation facility to find here on this rather bleak moor. The skyline ahead was a knobbly, undulating silhouette against the silver-grey of the sky. A huge rounded tump with a massive craggy face and extensive screes sweeping down to the mountain wall to my left was Manod Mawr. Borrow wrote of this terrain: " The country for some way east of Ffestiniog is very wild and barren, consisting of huge hills without trees or verdure." Well, this was in fact the edge of the moor known as Migneint which, to my eye, does not have huge hills.

I crossed the main spur to look down into the next valley called Cwm Cynfal, which was deeply cut and contained a pleasing arrangement of stream, vegetation and rock. The cwm's far slopes were laden with patchy coniferous forest; the near slope bright green and sheep-cropped; patches of rushes and marsh grass speckled the slope leading down to the stream. The valley closed in, hereabouts, for a rock face on the far side approached the cwm at right angles then turned to form the far side of a gorge down which the stream ran. I paused to admire the rugged scene from a view-point in a lay-by on the road, which had been constructed with money from the Rees Jeffreys Road Fund (1872-1954). The rocky gorge contained three spectacular waterfalls, the Rhaeadr y Cwm, which tumble down the precipitous canyon, visible only from this one point on the road.

Beyond the falls, the hillside was gorse, bracken and heather with patches of scree but, in contrast, on this side there was a flat meadow between the waterfalls and the road. Borrow was evidently equally taken with this view of what he'd been told was called Ceunant Comb (Hollow Dingle Cwm)* for he waxed lyrical with: "The valley is fresh and green and the lower parts of the hills on its farther side are, here and there, adorned with groves.At the eastern end is a gorge or ravine down which tumbles a brook in a succession of small cascades."

Above the top waterfall lay a green plateau where the stream was placid, gently meandering through the meadows and swishing round the boulders, glinting and glimmering in the sun. This country, up on the moor, up on the plateau, was gentle, less rugged. The colours of the hillsides had changed to the dun brown of moorland; the fertile greens of the valley didn't exist at this height of over 300m. I passed the milestone which informed me that Bala was 14 miles: a rather daunting jot of information!

At 9.30 I approached the road junction at Pont yr Afon Gam where, to my delight, I found that the building at the road junction had an unexpected 'cafe' sign on the wall. Well, I really could use a cuppa after the 200 metre ascent from Llan Ffestiniog. As I noisily approached the gate, the kitchen blind went up and I gestured "Any chance of a drink?" with my elbow and eyebrows. She beckoned me in, appeared at the door, and I said, "Could I have some tea?". She replied," Well, we don't open until ten but if you've walked up the hill, you deserve one." So the charming young north-country lass made me a large mug of tea, with rather more sugar than I normally take, and talked to me of this and that while I slurped it down. This young couple had been there five years, running the cafe in this isolated spot and were still renovating the building. It used to be an inn at the junction of two drovers' roads, I was told among a lot of other stuff that I was too thirsty to pay much attention to. I can't remember ever having been so appreciative of a cup of tea. My offer to pay for my drink was refused but I left some money under a magazine anyway for I thought that this must be a hard way to earn a living; a very short season and a bleak life in the winter. And a young couple deserved all the help they could get with such and enterprise. I left at about ten o'clock with best wishes for a good walk. What hospitality!

A bit further on, I came across signs of human life, of which, it must be said, there was not a lot of up on 'The Migneint' moor. A Land Rover was parked at the road edge hitched to a long trailer for carrying a vehicle. I heard the sound of an engine on the hill to my left and there, buzzing to and fro like an angry wasp was a quadbike, with sheepdogs in attendance, busy rounding up sheep. Evidently no more Shank's pony and shepherd's crook for the hill-farmer hereabouts for increased wealth, or subsidies, allowed the purchase of Land Rovers and quad bikes.

Borrow was fairly scathing about the Migneint for he wrote: "Nothing could be conceived more cheerless than the scenery around. The ground on each side of the road was mossy and rushy - no houses - instead of them were peat stacks, here and there, standing in their blackness. Nothing living to be seen except a few miserable sheep picking the wretched herbage or lying panting on the shady side of the peat clumps." Not much has changed since then except that peat-cutting no longer takes place. Me, I wouldn't have thought that sheep had the facial capability to look miserable.

I progressed into the peace of the high, gently undulating, boggy gound of the Migneint moor where one really would not want to set foot off the road for fear of disappearing into the mire. The peace was shattered, now and again, by the howling scream of jets from RAF Valley hurtling through the sky, barely higher than the surrounding hilltops.. I was ducking with the sudden shock of the noise and speed of these fearsome machines of war. Some lines from RL Stevenson helped to restore my equilibrium:

> "yet shall your ragged moor receive
>   the incomparable pomp of eve,
> and the cold glories of the dawn
>   behind your shivering trees be drawn"

Despite the forecast, I enjoyed blue sky, high cumulus and no rain. Boggy moorland stretched to a distant line of pylons. Since leaving the cafe, I'd seen no-one save the quadbike operator and a BT employee snoozing in his van at the roadside. The high skyline of the Arenigs, Fach a double summit on my left and Fawr to the right, like a lesser version of Moel Siabod, came into sight. This was the Migneint; this was Welsh high moorland and not the most interesting terrain; miles of undulating bog stuffed with reeds, marsh grass, cotton grass, brown grassland, poor grazing land and so not well populated with sheep. The only dry areas in this elevated sponge were little grass knolls with boulders and bracken. I wondered how the road had been constructed on such soft and boggy ground.

The featureless moor was at least a natural feature of the landscape and full of nature's natural curves: the skyline, the hillocks, the stream beds, the road itself, all undulating and sinuous. And then I came to the Forestry Commission plantation at spot height 419 on the lower slopes of Carnedd Iago. This presented itself as a repugnant, closely planted, dark green block imposed by man on the landscape with no regard for natural contours. The ruler-straight borders of the spruce wood stretched uphill and along the road edge; no attempt had been made to soften the impact of this alien vegetation; no deciduous trees grew along the margins. Dominating the backdrop were Moel Llyfnant to the right and to its left Arenig Fawr, separated by a wide cwm choked with more coniferous plantations.

There was worse to come for I soon found that the whole of the lower slopes of Carnedd Iago were forested, right down to the road, but not shown on my map. From this point, at Pont Nant y Lladron, or thereabouts, Borrow had glimpsed the gleam of water of Llyn Tryweryn which is nowadays invisible due to more coniferous woodland on the south side of the road. He wrote: "I saw something which appeared to be a sheet of water at the bottom of a low ground on my right. It looked far off." He decided to "go and see what it was". His wording is peculiar here because water looks like water to most people. Anyway, he made a detour to it and rested on its banks musing about the 'afanc' reputedly a creature "monstrous and horrible". I did not visit the lake for I had no desire to fight my way through repulsive sitka spruce for 800m, nor did I wish to visit the A4212, nor did I wish to struggle through the bog and tussock grass that would be underfoot! Borrow wrote of having some difficulty regaining the road, and I'm not surprised.

Later the coniferous plantation became more diffuse, with clearings, the trees not in straight lines or planted uniformly densely, but interspersed with some ash and oak. I was saddened, as always, to see that the road, the B4391, was littered along its verges with coke bottles, crisp bags, beer cans, expanded polystyrene fast-food containers and all the other trash that people throw out of their cars. Could one never escape the foul habits of modern man? Why does the motorist consider that the tidyness of his vehicle interior is more important than the countryside, which all passers-by will see? Chucking litter out of cars seemed even crasser up here in this wild, unpolluted country than elsewhere. I was further disgusted to see an enormous cardboard box, from a Phillips 28" colour TV and a similar carton for a Sony VCR thrown down at the side of the road.

Just before eleven o'clock I stopped at spot height 459 metres, the highest point on the road and my highest of the day, for a drink and a snack. I paused, however, for only quarter of an hour, crouched under my umbrella out of the rain, because within three minutes the midges had found me. It was typical midge country: boggy ground, damp air, no wind, in between the conifers, and there was warm, salty meat to bite. Borrow didn't mention midges. Were they not there in his day or did he travel so fast, without stopping, that they couldn't keep up with him? I admired the classic scarp and dip slopes of the summit of Arenig Fach, and the craggy, rotund hill and summit ridge of Arenig Fawr. The road bore very little traffic, the odd car from time to time, and there was certainly no-one on bike or foot. Not one of the few vehicles that passed offered me a lift.

I came to a fine, twentieth century, stone bridge over the substantial stream of Afon Taihirion which was evidently a modern replacement for the ancient, single-arched packhorse-type bridge that spanned the stream just uphill. The latter was mossy, disused, sprouting grass and somewhat sad but proud of its age and strength. Hereabouts Borrow wrote: "I was now almost choked with dust and thirst, and longed for nothing in the world so much as for water; suddenly I heard its blessed sound, and perceived a rivulet on my left hand. It was crossed by two bridges, one immensely old and terribly dilapidated, the other old enough but in better repair - I went and drank under the oldest bridge of the two. The water tasted of the peat of the moors, nevertheless I drank greedily of it, for one must not be over-delicate upon the moors." This is certainly something I wouldn't have done unless the stream was immediately spring-fed. There are dead sheep and all kinds of other nasty pollutants lying about on the hills and I'd suffered severe gastric upsets in the past after drinking from hill streams.

I was soon approaching the valley of the Afon Tryweryn. A quarry loomed at the foot of Arenig Fawr and faintly came the invasive roar of a tractor mowing in the fields a little way ahead at Tai Hirion, which was named as such on my map. The pastures of Tai Hirion between this road and the A4212, formed a narrowing triangle as the roads converged and appeared to have been mowed for hay. But as I came abreast of Tai Hirion* I saw that the tractor was not mowing grass but reeds, but for what purpose I did not know. The meadows had evidently been neglected for they were thick with reeds and thistles and marsh grass, leaving little grazing for sheep. Rams with huge curled horns started away from the roadside fence as I passed. Borrow stopped here and spoke to a "respectable-looking woman" who told him that the buildings were called Tai Hirion Migneint and dated 1630. They then spoke of Oliver Cromwell, the two bridges over the Afon Taihirion and of Llyn Tryweryn.

I could speak to no-one for the buildings at Tai Hirion no longer exist, but a grove of trees, and some collapsed stone walls marks their location At eleven forty I came to the deserted A4212, looked in both directions and stepped onto the tarmac. Hardly had I done so when the roar of tyres announced the approach of a car coming down the hill toward me, very fast indeed. As I scuttled ignominiously across the road, rucksack-laden, he accelerated and held down his horn, then passed behind me in a blaring thunder of sound. A failed attempt at homicide! What was the point in frightening me and doing a dangerous manoeuvre such as that ? Incomprehensible, lethal and moronic behaviour. Do motorists feel agressive and resentful guilt towards walkers? Are they so stupid and bored that they have to make walkers rush, without dignity, out of their way? Is it another instance of power-crazed lunatics with nothing in their heads?

I took the lane directly opposite which was the minor road to Bala. There was meadow-sweet on the river flats where meadow pipits and stonechats flew amongst the swirling insects. I soon came to the bridge over the Afon Tryweryn called Pont Rhyd y Fen* which arched over the sparkling little river in its level valley. Here were buttercups and fool's parsley in thick abundant clumps which gave the place a true feel of lowland country, but at 346m it was hardly that. Large beech trees overshadowed the lane, dominated by the sizzling crackle from the high tension overhead cables carrying power from Trawsfynydd to Bala. Borrow had come to a few houses just here, though none existed now, "on the margin of a meadow or fen in a valley through which the way trended to the east". He stopped and, once again, insouciantly asked for ale. This he drank and discovered that the place was called 'Rhyd y Fen' or the ford across the fen. So the bridge had not existed in the 1850s and the word 'pont' was added later.

It was a soft and mellow country; a far cry from the austere monochrome of the Migneint just a couple of kilometres behind me. The lane was steeped in that evocative scent of meadow-sweet in the warm air of the valley, quite a contrast from the sweet distinctive odour of fresh bracken that I'd stirred up by walking through it yesterday. As I approached the barren cliffs and terraces of the disused quarry, the old railway from Llan Ffestiniog to Bala was evident. Some redundant stone abutments straddling the road were testimony to the existence, at one time, of a tramway from the quarry to the nearby railway. I passed a grove of stunted, ancient, gnarled blackthorn trees, which could be mistaken for olive trees. Vetch, seeding grasses, foxglove and big spiny thistles brimming over with purple flowers decorated the road verges. Some boulders, loosened by I knew not what, thundered down the massive scar of the tiered quarry faces. Above the quarry, a steep mountainside of crags and turf led up to the summit of Arenig Fawr, truly a proper mountain. Borrow wrote of Arenig Fawr: " Of all the hills which I saw in Wales none made a greater impression upon me."

Shortly after a small hamlet I topped a rise and the reservoir of Llyn Celyn came into view: a huge sheet of water, calm and blue-grey, The water level was low, for about 15 feet of silt was visible round the sweeping shoreline. This didn't bode too well for water supplies later in the summer, or next winter. To the north of the lake rose low hills with featureless undulating skylines; to the south the huge bowl of the cwm containing Lyn Arenig Fawr.

Borrow reports meeting two groups of people to talk to on this road. I was less lucky - I only met one group and they were not locals. At around twelve thirty, near Bryn Ifan, I met a group of six teenagers doing their Duke of Edinburgh Award expedition. They didn't know exactly where they'd come from nor, it seemed, exactly where they were going. But they weren't letting such small considerations spoil their enjoyment of the day. It was pleasing to see young people backpacking, making a physical effort, using maps, finding their way and laughing through the countryside.

At one o'clock I stopped for lunch at a high spot on the road where the interesting view was now east, rather than north. It was a view of the sun- dappled hills across Bala lake, ruined by a monstrous pylon, directly in front of me; an intrinsically very ugly lattice-work of grey girders soaring into the sky, carrying six power cables. This steel leviathan definitely spoiled the view, but I never heard anyone complaining about these eyesores ruining the beauty of the countryside. But people do object vehemently to wind turbines which are far more attractive structures, gently moving in a static landscape, consuming nothing and producing no pollutants but serving society's need for electricity.

It began to rain as I hoisted myself to my feet and so the umbrella came into use. Borrow also used an umbrella on the apparently rare occasion that it rained during his long walk. He wrote a short eulogy to the umbrella in chapter 71 of 'Wild Wales' from which I quote: "Oh, how a man laughs who has a good umbrella when he has the rain at his back, aye and over his head too. Oh, what a good friend to man is an umbrella in rain time, and likewise at many other times". He then goes on to describe the uses of the gamp for repelling dogs and bulls and footpads and for establishing an air of respectability when ordering ale or seeking conversation with strangers. "Oh, a tent, a shield, a lance and a voucher for character is an umbrella". I have to agree with him on all these points except the last. It was my experience that a walker in the countryside with an umbrella would be considered eccentric, if not barmy, and viewed with some suspicion!

I passed some farm buildings painted matt green. This was a rare example of environmental sensitvity which I'd never seen before and which was visually a huge improvement on the usual shiny grey of modern farm buildings. They were almost unnoticeable in the green landscape; how refreshing. Did the local planners here actually have an environmentally sympathetic attitude to the colour of these massive buildings in the countryside?

Borrow stopped hereabouts for he wrote: "I arrived at a very small and pretty village in the middle of which was a tollgate - seeing an old woman seated at the door of the gatehouse, I asked her the name of the village".She said it was called Tref y Talcot or the Village of the Tollgate.

With this in mind as I came to the name sign for the village of Llidiardau, I persuaded myself that the stone-built ruin by the road-side just next to the sign was the old toll-house*. It certainly had a buttress on the front whose purpose, if not to support a toll-gate, was difficult to imagine. The village itself was certainly small but no longer sufficiently pretty to remark upon. The village school was remotely sited some mile or so further on and just beyond the road junction at Tyn y Sarn. At this point I was about three miles from Bala and it is likely that Borrow paused here, at the same distance from the town, to admire the view of a valley to the south-west of the road. He wrote: "Shortly after leaving the village of the tollgate I came to a beautiful valley. On my right hand was a river the farther bank of which was fringed with trees; on my left was a gentle ascent, the lower part of which was covered with yellow luxuriant corn; a little farther on was a green grove, behind which rose up a moel." A little further on he was informed by some carters that he was three miles from Bala.

Southwards I could now see the rocky ramparts of Cader Idris, a high, whalebacked, grey, long, notched summit which was now in the clouds: the rain clouds of the storm that had recently wetted my umbrella. I soon entered the village of Rhyd Uchaf, where my first impressions were not good due to the scruffy council houses in a square. Caravans and rusting vehicles were parked around the square and the children's playground was littered with dog excrement. Christmas lights festooned a house nearby, ready to be lit up in December, or, doubtless, much earlier. Beyond the Talybont Methodist Chapel (1810 - 1937) I stopped and spoke to two women who were, a rare sight, chatting at the side of the road. They were merely sheltering from the rain, or so they said, even though it had stopped thirty minutes earlier!

So I asked the two women 'sheltering from the rain' if they knew anywhere hereabouts that used to be called, or was still called, Tref y Talcot. The were most interested in my expedition, both had Borrow's book, and they debated the matter for a while. When I mentioned, as an afterthought, that this translated as 'The village of the tollgate' one said, " Well, perhaps that was the old name for Llydiardau, which means 'gates' in Welsh". Aha, did that confirm my belief in the stone ruin? It was all a tad uncertain so they suggested that I should ask the bookseller in Bala who was something of a local historian.

By three o'clock I was coming down the hill, in the rain, into Bala. The town didn't look too promising as I entered it. There was an unpleasant rash of council flats to the left and an ugly, 1960s, school to the right but the impact of these was mellowed somewhat by the elegance of a slender and well-proportioned church spire beyond. I turned right into the main street and made my way to the White Lion Hotel, which is the inn that Borrow stayed at on his return to Bala after re-visiting Llangollen. He described the coffee-room as presenting "an agreeable contrast to the gloomy, desolate places through which I had lately come".

The White Lion* is an imposing hostelry, ornately half -timbered on the first floor, situated in the centre of the main street. It had recently been redecorated, inside and outside where the walls are a sparkling white, but the date 1759 is still evident on the front facade. I was rather disappointed, therefore, to find that my room - room number one and doubtless the only single room in the hotel- was old-fashioned, containing some tired-looking furniture, a rather utilitarian bed, a brown carpet, threadbare in places, flaking paintwork and grimy window glass. I was also sad to see that the bedding consisted of sheets and blankets, as it had done in the Black Boy at Caernarfon whereas at Ffestiniog and Beddglert I had slept under a duvet. But the room was clean, and I was in no state to be critical!

Bala was a frenetically busy town, even at six in the evening with much more traffic than you'd expect. In search of a book to read, I soon found that there was nowhere to buy a good read, in English. There were cheap romances for sale in one or two shops but I did finally track down an Alexander Kent in the Post Office. There was certainly a noticeable Welsh sub-culture in evidence for my hotel room contained Murroughs Welsh Brew Tea (blended and packed in Wales), Dwyfor Coffee (freeze dried Colombian) and Dwyfor Luxury Chocolate Drink (Diod Siocled Poeth). In the shops there was plenty of Welsh to be heard and there were Welsh books, postcards, posters, leaflets and much pre-packed food labelled in Welsh.

In the pub where I took my evening meal I heard no English spoken by the local people and there was a choice of Welsh ales: Brains, Rev. Jenkins and Robinsons. I had been told earlier in the day that about half of the local people were Welsh speakers, and therefore locally born and educated for it is usually too much effort for incomers to learn the language. Try as I might, I could find no-one of middle-age in the pub or the hotel who seemed inclined to tell me if they knew anything of Bala in the 1850s - indeed most of the denizens seemed to be under the age of 30 and not at all interested in, or knowledgeable, about such matters.

The manager of the Welsh antiquarian bookshop greeted me in Welsh, of course, and was then very helpful when I enquired, in English, about the possible location of the village that Borrow called Tref y Talcot. However, he could find out nothing then and there but said that he would research the matter in due course.

In Bala at 9pm the local rowdy youths were beginning to shout, laugh, swear and vomit in the High Street. My room, though set back slightly from the main frontage of the hotel nevertheless faced directly onto the main street so I took the full brunt of the evening's delinquent shenanigans. I'd never thought that I'd need earplugs on such a trip but I could have done with them that night, and again later in the walk as time would show.

***

The letter 'y' in Welsh is pronounced as 'ee' at the end of words as a general rule. Where it occurs within a word then the sound is 'uh' as in 'upper'. So 'Cymru' sounds as 'come-ree"

The diphthong 'ae' sounds like the 'i' in 'mice' so 'maes' (meaning 'place') is in fact 'mice'!

The diphthong 'au' sounds like 'ah-ee" (quickly).

The diphthong 'eu' sounds like 'oi-ee" (quickly).

The letters 'si' together sound as 'sh'.

The Moelwyns

The pylon on the Migneint

Llanuwchllyn station

The pass, Bwlch y Groes, from the south

THE HIGHEST PASS AND THE BABY DOVEY

Breakfast at the hotel was the usual rather uninspiring meal the main component of which was once again the full British breakfast which I eschewed for cereals and scrambled egg. As I ate I mused that Borrow reported a breakfast at this hotel of " a pot of hare, ditto of trout, pot of prepared shrimps, dish of plain shrimps, tin of sardines, beautiful beefsteak, eggs, muffin, large loaf and butter, not forgetting capital tea". Well, how our habits and expectations have changed, and not for the better.

After smearing my toes with vaseline and shrugging my way into my rucksack straps, I left the hotel at eight-thirty.

The sky was, again, solidly and greyly overcast with nary enough blue for the proverbial sailor's trousers. At the northern end of Lake Bala, the placid lake, well ensconced between the hills, stretched away to the south. The wooded slopes on either side were hardly reflected in the fog-murk coloured water. The serenely bobbing small yachts nevertheless lent it all a summery air. I turned right at the lake's corner and passed the yacht club.

I soon found myself walking next to the single, narrow-gauge line of the Bala Lake Railway. A poster announced that the first train would be at 11.10 and that four trains would run today. Along this four miles of lakeside road there were hay fields, deciduous woods, hedges full of summer flowers, dog roses, ash, hazel, hawthorn, beech, and the ubiquitous bracken and nettles. By half-past nine the sun was shining on the lake, which now reflected a gleam of light onto the dark hills beyond. Cader Idris rose massively behind the lake; jagged, ragged hills stretched all the way to its end.

This was the very best of mellow lake and hill landscapes, with that feel of rural peace and permanence that rises from an aged land, well-worked and well-loved by those who inhabit it. And the land certainly did seem well-tended for all was lush and green amongst the tidy fields and neat farmhouses set in that sublime mixture of variegated woodland, meadowland and bracken-blanketed hillside.

At Llangower I passed an ugly outbreak of yellow-brick council housing and crossed an ancient bridge only twelve feet narrow. Stone cottages were dotted along the lane; a stone chapel crouched in a grassy unkempt graveyard where one inscription read *"Here lies the body of Moses Jones of Bala who died aged 68 on March 8 1812"*. The squire's mansion at the village's end was hidden deep behind bush and hedge. Elderflower and honeysuckle tangled the hedgerows of a lane so quiet that I could hear one blackbird singing for at least ten minutes as I paced along. At nine forty-five I paused at the railway halt of Pentre Piod where a short platform and a small shelter were painted in the old GWR livery of dark brown and cream.

At ten o'clock, just before the turn off up the valley of Afon Twrch, I stopped to look down on the station at Llanuwchllyn*. Four pretty little maroon and cream carriages were waiting at the platform coupled to a small green diesel shunter. A trim signal-box in brick with maroon and cream paintwork, stood close by. The 'stationscape' was so litter free and carefully polished, so neatly painted and bedecked with brilliant blobs of geranium flowers that I thought with disgust of the dirty, litter-strewn, weedy and seedy shambles that is Hereford station in these days of privatisation, profit and uncaring service. Imposing stone houses, looking cheerful and bright and colourful, comprised the village, beyond the immaculate station.

The landlord at the White Lion had told Borrow that the "greater part" of the route to Dinas Mawddwy was "very rough, over hills and mountains, belonging to the great chain of Arran, which constituted, upon the whole, the wildest part of all Wales". This description was perhaps rather overstated but the valley of the Twrch did turn out to be remote and isolated.

When I arrived at the beginning of this "greater part", the road up the Twrch valley bore a sign displaying *"Single track road with few passing places, weight limit 2 tons, unsuitable for caravans"*. Well, that won't affect me, I thought, except that it may be largely traffic free, so I started up the hill road, optimistically. It was uphill steeply, immediately, with a fine view of the handsome little peak of Moel Ddu. This hill was rocky at the top of a steep ridge and seemed to be worthy of a scramble if I was ever passing again. But not today, oh dear me, no.

I came to Pont Afon Fechan*, where I believe Borrow "crossed a bridge over a deep gully which discharged its waters into a river in a valley on the right". Some semi-detached stone cottages crouched by the stream; the road was deserted: no traffic, no pedestrians. The hillside swept down from the road to the enchanting Afon Twrch which meandered its babbling way along the valley through small copses of ash and oak. Beyond, the tree-studded hillside give way to the bracken and rock of Moel Ddu. Above the road was typical sheep pasture: short-shorn grassland abundant with uncut thistles, old walls, banks and boulders, bracken and brambles, ash and alder all in an attractive and pleasing random array. The farm at Coed Ladyr was, sadly, derelict: yet more indications of an abandoned countryside.

Borrow wrote: "I wandered on over much rough ground till I came to a collection of houses at the bottom of a pass leading up a steep mountain". This hamlet was, I think, Talardd* where I found some cottages, and a neglected bungalow on the hillside, placed at a stream junction where the steep-sided Cwm Croes met the Twrch valley. Borrow's description fitted this place, and the road did steepen perceptibly here. As was his habit, Borrow spoke to a resident and was told that the place was named Ty Capel Saer, or the House of the Chapel of the Carpenter, but I could see no sign of any building that might have been a chapel nor was there anyone in the hamlet to ask and no carpenters in sight.

The postman's van passed me for the third time that morning but it was the only vehicle I'd seen since leaving the end of Lake Bala. Shortly after eleven I came to Ty Nant* where Borrow once again knocked on the door and enquired about the name of the house. The "smiling young woman" who opened the door told him it was Ty Nant or the house of the dingle and that she spoke no English. Ty Nant was now a modern sheep farm with gigantic steel barns in a farmyard milling with sheep kicking up such a din of baas that I didn't hear a dung-splattered tractor that was doing its best to mow me down. Leviathan tractors and trailers stood in the yard and hid the stone farmhouse at the back. The gates to the yard were closed and padlocked and machinery was buzzing in a shed. It was no longer the welcoming Ty Nant where lived the smiling young woman who "looked the picture of kindness".

By eleven-thirty I was entering the upper Twrch valley, known as Cwm Cynllwydd, which Borrow found out from a woman at Ty Capel Saer and which he translated as meaning 'hoary-headed". This was a seriously steep ascent, with a gradient of about 1 in 20. I toiled up the grade, sweat dripping from my forehead onto my boots, past a deep gully, to get above the tree line, onto open hillside where the upper Twrch valley appeared as a spectacular semicircle of a green bowl, ringed with hills. Two farms littered the bottom of the bowl, both with hideous modern grey, hard-edged barns and sheds, linked by a meandering lane: geometric blots on a soft and gentle landscape. Between the farms were lines of trees, hedgerows and small fields of grazing land which contrasted with the khaki hillside and the bare and level skyline above the little flawed paradise below. It was view to savour, notwithstanding man's ugly intrusions. I was at grid reference 912250.

I sweated on, humped under my rucksack, up the unremittingly steep road. To distract myself from my bodily discomforts I noted that at one farm there were five vehicles, three of which were 4x4s, a tractor, and a horse box all parked near to two new barns, an older farm barn and the farmhouse. The other farm had no vehicles at all. There was a chaos of sheep in the in-by for dipping, maybe, for they'd all been recently shorn.

Borrow "proceeded and after a considerable time reached the top of the pass." No mention of the appalling steep ascent then. Did he not sweat, was he not plagued by flies, did he observe nothing hereabouts?

Higher up there were broken rock slabs stuck into hillside at improbable angles, shaly-schisty rock which to Borrow would have been " awsome and lofty", but he doesn't mention them. I paused from sweaty effort to admire the fine view, back down the U-shaped valley, of all the way I'd come from Llanuwchllyn, and beyond the valley's end the huge purple mass of the double summit of Cader Idris, its ridges dropping away on either side of the notched top.

By eleven forty-five I could see the summit of the road at Bwlch y Groes, still a long and steep way up but now at least within sight. The long serrated ridge of the Arrans rose, remotely, beyond the rim of the semicircular bowl. Here was a true sense of remoteness, really wild Wales and, save for the greenness of the upper Twrch valley, the immediate landscape was very similar to the Migneint of yesterday. I plodded my way past a conifer plantation about twenty years old just near the re-entrant at grid reference 915239 which was not shown on my aged one-inch map. Here and there I could see that the road was nothing more than a thin layer of tarmac laid over the old rough stone surface of the drovers' road that Borrow had walked.

With a gasp for breath, and of relief, I reached the col, Bwlch y Groes*, just before midday. It had been a long, steep haul to reach this, at 546 metres (1791 feet), the highest road pass in Wales. and the highest point on the whole route. The information board in the little car park at the pass included the following :

"The pass used to be the pilgrims' route from north-west Wales to St David's in the south. A little way down the pass is a cross placed there as a symbol of faith and strength which has comforted lonely travellers since mediaeval times. In 1989 pilgrims replaced the original cross with the one that stands there today. The thick black lines on the lower slopes of the Arrans are the edges of peat bogs and a rare sight these days. If you had been standing here in the 1920s and 1930s you would have been in danger of being run over for Austin's test drivers used this road to test their cars. An English driver named this place 'Hellfire Pass' but the local population returned it to its original name of Bwlch y Groes."

I enjoyed the very fine panoramic view down the Twrch valley to the plain of Lake Bala and the most exposed view of the dark and craggy flanks of Cader Idris that one can see from anywhere. To the left of Cader, the hills of the Lleyn Peninsula were dimly visible in the sea-haze. I relished the spectacular view of the Arran ridge, dark now for the sun had gone again, high, gullied, a broad grassy ramp sweeping down from the level summit ridge, the wildness of the abundant rock, and, in the middle ground, the drab-brown mounds of what may have been moraine.   As I mused at this point, the last verse of Gerard Manly Hopkins' 'Inversnaid' came into my mind:

> "What would the world be, once bereft
> of wet and wildness? let them be left
> O let them be left, wildness and wet;
> long live the weeds and the wilderness yet"

I did not, however, enjoy the arrival of three cars which roared up the road from the other side, wheeled into the car-park spraying stones at my shins, paused momentarily then rushed off down the hill up which I had laboured. Out for a drive, I supposed, but not for the scenery, evidently.

On the pass Borrow commented: "From thence I had a view of the valley and lake of Bala, the lake looking like an immense sheet of steel. A round hill, however, somewhat intercepted the view of the latter". I should say it did because the lake was not visible at all from the pass. A bit more artistic licence, methinks. He went on: "The scene in my immediate neighbourhood was very desolate; moory hillocks were all about me of a wretched russet colour; on my left, on the very crest of the hill up which I had so long been toiling stood a black pyramid of turf, a pole on the top of it". Ah, at last an admission that he too had toiled! The pole on the top of Moel y Gerrig Duon is no longer there, though the summit itself is distinctive enough. He then commented, wrongly, that the road now went due west, which it does not; it goes south from the pass.

I dropped down the hill to get out of the chilly wind to find somewhere sheltered to sit and drink some more orange juice. I'd bought juice as I was fed up with drinking water all day, every day, but regretted it because it was heavier than water and didn't quench the thirst to the same extent. No more orange juice, then, but perhaps I'd try milk instead tomorrow. Stretched before me was a very different landscape. A vast, olive-green, concave, undulating plateau sloped gently up to the skyline and, to the right, suddenly dropped away, with an abrupt change of colour and of slope, to become a shaly escarpment. This precipitous slope was blanketed in that matt brown of heather before it comes into flower in August; patches of fine scree interrupted the heather blanket; some low crags of bare rock frilled the edge of the scarp. There were a few cars groaning up the hill to the col but no walkers, no cyclists, no-one to talk to.

Of the view from the southern side of the bwlch Borrow wrote: "The pass down which I was now going was yet wilder than the one up which I had lately come. Close on my right was the steep hill's side out of which the road or path had been cut, which was here and there overhung by crags of wondrous forms; on my left was a very deep glen, beyond which was a black, precipitous, rocky wall, from a chasm near the top of which tumbled with a rushing sound a slender brook seemingly the commencement of a mountain stream which hurried into a valley far below towards the west".

After twenty minutes' rest, which I thought I deserved after the long ascent, I got up ready to step it out in no uncertain style down the hill. However, I soon found that going down was as painful as coming up. The road, only ten feet wide, sloped downwards at a gradient of 17%, crippingly steep, pulling at my ankles and cramping my thighs. Shortly I could see the junction with the road from Lake Vyrnwy where two motorcyclists were having a break, sitting on the roadside wall next to two large, shiny sports bikes. They ignored me as I approached but, undaunted by this spurning of a mere pedestrian, I asked, "Are you going far?"

"Don't reckon we're going nowhere, chum," came the reply from the burly bloke, "'er bike's on the blink. Wouldn't come up the 'ill. Kept losin' power." At this I inspected the bike, and said, in the current vernacular, " Blimey, you've got plenty of power there; issa Honda 600, innit?" She said," Yeah, you'd fink so, woonchew, but we neerly 'ad to pushit, load of junk". He said, "Musta bin the 'ill, too steep, juice not feedin' inta the carb. Gotta map? Enny more 'ills, are there?" I said that, as they were just below the highest road pass in Wales, they were unlikely to find anymore uphill stretches for a bit. I left them to their fags and muttered imprecations about the shortcomings of Japanese sports bikes and tottered off down the incline.

The pain of the descent was alleviated by the lovely view down the deep and verdant vale *(oops, shades of Borrowese creeping in here)* which wound round complex interlocking spurs. It was as mellow and beautiful a valley view as I'd seen anywhere in Wales. I'm amazed that Borrow doesn't comment on the valley view at all for his next remarks, after the quotation above, were not made until he reached the valley floor.

To complement the glorious surroundings there was birdsong from skylarks and rockpipits. Three wheatear fledglings, incompetent fliers, were fumbling and fluttering along the road verge before me as I descended whilst leaning back to combat the pull of gravity on the gradient. The view of the scarp slope improved as I lost height; it was all purple and green and pink and grey; long tongues and streaks of green bracken and browny-purple heather between the snakes of grey scree; deep erosion gullies incised with bright green lines of moisture.

I came down eventually, walking comfortably on the grazed road verge, to oak and ash trees standing amidst thickets of gorse, which was not in flower, so kissing was out of season. I negotiated a hairpin bend and strode down to the valley floor. Just here the flat meadowland swept away from the road to make an amphitheatre enclosed by soaring steep slopes and crags down the centre of which a broken waterfall dropped from an invisible valley above. What was it called in school geography? Ah yes, a hanging valley, that's it. Beyond and higher, the skyline was a mountain ridge. I paused to inspect the map and familiarise myself with this new country. The ridge was evidently that of the summits of Aran Fawddwy and Aran Benllyn, the waterfall was the infant River Dovey in the early stages of its journey from its source at Craiglyn Dyfi, just below the summit of Fawddwy, to the sea at Aberdovey.

Of exactly this scene Borrow wrote: "On my right a black, gloomy, narrow valley or glen showed itself; two enormous craggy hills of immense altitude, one to the west and the other to the east of the entrance; that to the east terminating in a peak. The background to the north was a wall of rocks forming a semicircle, something like a bent bow with the head downward; behind this bow just in the middle, rose the black loaf of Arran. A torrent tumbled from the lower part of the semicircle, and after running for some distance to the south turned to the west, the way I was going." Hum, Borrow really should have abandoned use of the points of the compass for the two Aran summits are to the west, to the north lies Tap Nyth yr Eryri, and the infant Dovey runs south all the way.

He turned into the "gloomy vale" and spoke to two men at a house called Ty Mawr. They discussed the source of the Dovey, the possibility of the lake containing crocodiles, or afanc, and the hill called Tap Nyth yr Eryri. This was an amusing exchange for Borrow asked, in Welsh, if the younger man had ever been up Tap Nyth but received no answer. "He no care for your question," said the older man; "ask him price of pig." Borrrow did so whereupon the young man's face brightened and he not only answered the question but told him that he had a fat hog to sell. "Ha, ha," said the old man, "he plenty of Welsh now, for he see reason. To other question he no Welsh at all, no more than English, for he see no reason. What business he on Tap? His business down in sty with pig."

I peered into the amphitheatre but could see no sign of a 'big house', then continued past a mucky farm littered with plastic detritus and an overflowing reeking slurry pool to the unattractive modern bridge at Aber Rhiwlech*. The bridge, which Borrow mentions, spanned the stream coming down from Bwlch y Groes.

It was now one o'clock and, in need of a rest, I paused to gawp at the astonishing steepness and greenness of the hills surrounding the Dovey valley; on the map the contours of the encompassing hills were almost touching each other. There was a good deal of bare rock around on these hillsides too, to such an extent that there looked to be the possibility of some good scrambling on the aretes of Tap Nyth and Darren Ddu. After the bridge, Borrow "soon came to a place where the two waters joined". Well, it wasn't the junction of these two waters, for that lay off the road and on the other side of the valley. Here Borrow found some-one else to talk to - goodness me, weren't there a lot of people around with the time and inclination to chew the fat? This time it was "a very sensible man" who believed that the Dovey actually originated on Bwlch y Groes.

I walked on down the quiet lane through a very pretty landscape. Uncut hedges hemmed the road, black cattle grazed on the meadows by the river. The view ahead was dominated by a circular grove of dark conifers centrally positioned on the very top of a bright green hillock. I thought of Alfred Watkins' concept of ley-lines and what a fine line-marker this mound would be.

Having drunk as much orange juice as I could stomach that morning, I stopped at a cottage in woodland, Bryn Awel dated 1863, and knocked on the door. A large man, with a friendly face and wearing an Environment Agency sweatshirt opened the door and I asked for some water. He agreed that I had a right to a considerable thirst if I'd come over Bwlch y Groes, departed and returned with bottled water. I said that tap water would be fine and he said that they didn't drink the tap water in the summer as it came off the hill and was often cloudy and bad-tasting. I offered to pay for the water, which he'd had to buy, but he refused my offer and said that it was a pleasure. More Welsh hospitality.

I moved on, breathing the heavenly scent of honeysuckle in full flower, admiring the deep cleft in the hills to the east, whose depths were be-diamonded by the sunlight on an intermittent cascade, to the village of Llanymawddwy which I reached about one-thirty. A stone-built church and old stone cottages nestled in the greenery and, surprisingly for such a small settlement, there was an information board with the message: *You are now standing on a drovers' road. These can be found throughout*

Wales and were used to drive cattle and other livestock to markets in England. The drovers then faced a perilous journey home with pockets full of money. This was the way to Bwlch y Groes and the road to Bala. This is a very spiritual place for pilgrims and drovers prayed here before tackling the pass. They needed somewhere to rest and there used to be seven public houses in this village with names linked to droving. Soldiers are reputed to have sharpened their swords on the font in the church before going to battle at the pass. The village is famous for its two giants; Llewellyn Fawr is buried in the churchyard here and it is said that bones twice the size of normal human remains were unearthed nearby. These are thought to belong to Cawel Fawddwy who threw a rock from the top of the Arans leaving indentations where his fingers held it."

In addition to the church there was the very small, square Bethesda Chapel, 1884, and beyond, an attractive collection of stone-built houses and cottages along the roadside. As it was Sunday, people were out and about, gardening, strolling, cleaning cars; in fact there was more human animation than I'd seen since leaving Bala. Borrow doesn't mention this village by name though he does comment:'I passed a village with a stupendous mountain just behind it to the north, which I was told was called Moel Vrith. I was now drawing near to the western end of the valley." In view of the latter remark, I suspect that he was at Llanerth, not at Llanymawddwy and I couldn't find anything called Moel Vrith on the map. Perhaps his appetite for hilly country had worn thin for he goes on, sardonically and rather feebly: " Scenery of the wildest and most picturesque description was rife and plentiful to a degree: hills were here, hills were there; some tall and sharp, other huge and lumpy; hills were on every side."

I left the village behind and walked on through the peace of the Dovey valley with occasional glimpses of the crystal waters of the river through the trees; through the appalling reek of muck-spreading; past increasingly frequent stone houses, all in good repair: I was obviously entering a more affluent area inhabited not by farmers but by working middle-class and retirees. I passed an old house needlessly named Ty'n y Fordd, or the house on the road. At two forty-five I reached Aber Cywarch, a small hamlet where some men were arguing in Welsh about the best way to start their tractor. Borrow asked a man galloping on horseback the name of this place, then exclaimed: " Aber Cywarch! Why, that's the place where Ellis Wynn composed his immortal Sleeping Bard, the book which I translated in the blessed days of my youth." The hamlet was at the mouth of Cwm Cywarch where I had passed many contented and demanding hours climbing on Craig Cywarch about twenty five years ago but I couldn't see into the Cywarch valley because of the dense growth of trees behind the village.

At Dinas Mawddwy*, ten minutes further on, Borrow remarked: " Dinas, though at one time a place of considerable importance, if we may judge from its name, which signifies a fortified city, is at present little more than a collection of filthy huts. Fierce-looking, red-haired men who seemed as if they might be descendants of the red-haired banditti of old, were staggering about, and sounds of drunken revelry echoed from the huts." These men would have been miners from the prolific lead mines and stone quarries of the area.

Borrow was pleased to leave Dinas and went on to find an inn at Mallwydd. As for me, I was in no condition to be so proud, being exhausted of energy and streaming with sweat, and so I stopped at the Red Lion at Dinas to ask for bed and breakfast. Unbelievably, in such an undistinguished place which was not situated anywhere in particular, they had no rooms. I took this in with mixed feelings: on one hand I was too fatigued to take any pleasure in walking further, on the other hand there was a peculiar, secretive atmosphere in the bar that made me not want to linger. I was given some rather confusing directions to the nearest bed and breakfast and staggered out back onto the road. Borrow was right in the sense that Dinas was still not an attractive place but there were no filthy huts in view! A kilometre further on the A470 I came to the Buckley Pines Hotel at Minllyn at about three-thirty and managed to secure a room, which was peaceful with a fine view of the Dovey. It was just as well for I could go no further. Ah, the benison of a bath full of hot water. Ah, the relief of being able to get my boots off. Ah, the pleasure of a cup of very sugary tea.

I was pleased that I'd stopped here because, though it was expensive for bed and breakfast, it was an interesting building and very tastefully decorated internally with many intriguing pieces of furniture and pictures, with an Asian or Turkish theme. Buckley Pines, built in 1873 by Sir Edmund Buckley MP, is the oldest reinforced concrete building in Europe and the second oldest known in the world. It's Grade 2 listed and was originally constructed with 52 windows - a fresh view every week of the year. (This was an odd fact and one which I had cause to remember later in the walk near Devil's Bridge). I heard no Welsh spoken in the bar where I rehydrated my dessicated body with several pints of Worthington and ate a passable vegetarian supper. Not having Borrow's social and conversational skills, I didn't engage the 'maid' in a lengthy dialogue, as he did, and even if there had been a 'maid' I doubt that the conversation would have been of much interest.

***

The ubiquitous 'Llan.....' prefix to many place names signifies a church, chapel or other sacred site or religious settlement. It often precedes the name of the saint who occupied the site. Thus 'Llangollen" means 'The Church of Saint Collen'.

The commonplace prefix 'Aber......' signifies the mouth of a stream or river or its confluence with another. It's often followed by the name of the river, so 'Abertawe' means the mouth of the river Tawe (and is in fact the Welsh name for Swansea). 'Aberafon' means the mouth of a river....name not specified...and there is a village with this name in S Wales.

AN INTERVIEW ON THE DROVERS' ROAD

For his journey southward to Machynlleth, Borrow trod the road on the eastern side of the Dovey valley which was probably the only road in the valley at that time. This is now the A470 and seething with hell-bent motorists and huge 44 tonne trucks carrying supermarket goods from depot to store at the behest of market forces. This would have been a horrific route to walk so, in the absence of any other feasible route, I followed the minor, unclassified road which ran parallel, on the west side of the valley.

Whilst perusing the map and reading Borrow's text for the next stage of the walk, I mused on how different it must have been for him, walking as he did without the benefit of a map. He had to discover the names of villages, valleys and mountains by asking local people and he was obviously often confused as to the direction and position of notable landmarks. Having left The Brigands Inn at Mallwyd , which is only a mile or so south of Minllyn, "a little way behind", he stopped to take a last view of the previous day's terrain. He refers to a mountain called Dinas, which can be identified on the OS map as being 478 metres high, but the another peak that he calls Cefn Coch I could not identify. He also describes a hill which he calls Pen Dyn which I also cannot identify even though he says that the Afon Gerist rises on its eastern side and the Maw on its west, for this topographical layout makes no sense on the map.

He walked on through Linau and over the bridge there, entered Cemmaes and stopped at an inn, which is now called The Penrhos Arms Hotel*. There follows, in his text, an amusing account of his experience with secretive locals who, when they found out that he spoke Welsh, shut up altogether and maintained a "suspicious silence". To aggravate them, Borrow then got out his notebook and began to write a long and detailed description of the kitchen in which he and the locals were sitting.

Silence prevailed whilst he did this. He then got up, left the inn and, fifty yards down the road, turned round to see the whole company of the kitchen standing outside the inn staring at him. He pulled out his notebook again, which was too much for the starers, who immediately bolted back into the hostelry.

As for me, with a less exciting day in prospect, I left the Buckley Pines at nine-forty on Sunday July 11 under cool overcast on the minor road to Aberangell. I pondered the various snippets of information I had gleaned at the hotel. As a family-run hotel the quality of the accommodation and the food and the service were far better than I'd had at, for instance, the Black Boy at Caernarfon or the White Lion at Bala. These two inns were operated by Welsh Historic Inns which is a hotel chain and not a tourist organisation, as I had thought. I had been advised not to stay at the Wynnstay Arms in Machynlleth, for it was expensive, but to look for a pink-painted bed and breakfast on the way into town. I was beginning to think that I might not get that far because I had a considerable blister on my right heel which was cramping my style somewhat.

The Dovey valley was vibrantly green even without sunshine and still enclosed by the softness of the hills on either side. Not much of Wild Wales hereabouts as the rurality was rather spoiled by some huge depots with attendant fork-lift trucks, here on the edge of Minllyn. I passed along the wooded lane, past well-manicured gardens and recent hay cutting in the fields, grateful not to have to walk on the main road whose traffic I could faintly hear. Here, there was no traffic on a Sunday morning and so it was pleasant walking which further diminished any desire I might have had to follow footpaths, even if there had been any leading in the right direction. The Dovey was no longer an infant river but now mature and shallow, meandering between tree-lined banks, calmly and peacefully. Sheep speckled the valley floor and the hill slopes with dots of white in great profusion.

The vale was wild only in the sense that the hedges were not cut and, as a result, huge foxgloves, tall willow herb, spreading bracken and frothy meadow-sweet arched over the road and narrowed its useable width. Some low rocky cliffs on either side of the river near an isolated stone cottage indicated a river canyon in the making.

As I walked, I pondered that it is remarkable how the subjects of conversation in bars have changed since Borrow's day. One doesn't imagine that the dialogues he reports are typical (or even entirely factual) but I compared his reported rather high-brow conversations with those I heard last night in the bar which had centred round the mundane subjects of motoring routes, petrol consumption, mobile phone tariffs and football.

At a quarter past ten I passed a pipe stuck into the roadside bank which spouted a stream of water into an ancient chipped cream enamel bowl with two green handles next to which proudly stood a slate sign engraved with the legend "Pistyll Ffriddfach". I supposed that this was some historic spring or water source, but the crudeness of the enamel bowl was at odds with the engraved slate slab. I passed several large houses, one of which had a vertically mounted sundial on the wall: a rare sight, especially in Wales. The line of the former railway could just be seen between road and river as a grassy track. A glance at the map showed that this line must have ended at Dinas, for it by-passed Mallwyd and most certainly wouldn't have gone over the 300m pass between Dinas and Dolgellau nor over Bwlch y Groes. Hmm, perhaps this line had been built to transport the products of the mines and quarries at Dinas Mawddwy in which Borrow's red-haired bandits worked.

The village of Aberangell boasted a tourist information board which announced:

" The village around you used to be a hive of activity. In the eighteenth and nineteenth centuries families either farmed or worked in the quarry which was four miles above the village and provided slate for the buildings in the area as well as places further afield. Transporting the slate became possible when the railway was built. (No date was given for this). To move the finished slate, a tramway was made from the quarry down

through the village and to the railway on the valley floor. Opposite, is the old post road built before the railway came to this part of Wales. It joined north and mid Wales and meant that the post and people could travel fast and more easily but, as travelling became more common, so did highway robbery. This stretch of the railway linked Dinas with the rest of the country. Sir Edmund Buckley built the railway which transported farm animals as well as slate slab for sale. It also meant that the villagers could have day trips by train to the seaside at Aberystwyth.which became a traditional family outing".

Ah, so my surmise about the railway was correct! And there's Sir Edmund Buckley again, he of the Buckley Pines Hotel. I wonder where his money came from.. I imagined that the tramway had been on the line of a lane that led up the valley of the Afon Angell. The map showed this to continue as a track up into the forestry plantations of the Dovey Forest. The map also showed several old quarries tucked amongst the convoluted contours high in the forest which were....yes, about four miles from the village.

Most of the houses in the village looked pre-Victorian so the place hadn't changed much since Borrow's day. Many houses were built of slate slab including the Horeb Chapel dated 1899 and the Bethania chapel built in 1902 which was a larger and more elaborate structure than the Horeb with smart yellow-stone arches round the windows and doors. There was a pleasing bridge over another clear mountain stream; this pretty little village had a definite village centre with bus-stop and post box and a satisfying mix of houses of different ages and styles. I passed another chapel which had been converted into a residence. What a lot of worshipping must have gone on here!

At the southern outskirts of the village I spied two elderly men leaning on the railings, enjoying the view of the river and chewing the fat. Ah, I thought, a conversation opportunity, and so I approached them, undaunted by hearing their Welsh dialogue.

Me: "Good morning gents, I hope I didn't startle you".

First man: "Good morning, I had a suspicion there was someone around, heh, heh".

Me: "I'm walking a route that an Englishman called George Borrow walked in 1854

First man: "Oh, yes, George Borrow, yes, I've read his book. I didn't know he walked down this way though".

Me: "Yes, he walked from Caernarfon down to Swansea but here he would have walked on the other side of the valley, on the main road".

First man: "And he stopped in Cemmaes like".

Me: "He did. There's an interesting account in his book of what happened to him at the inn at Cemmaes".

Second man: "Oh, yes".

Me: "Yes, he was making notes in his notebook and the people in the bar didn't like it because they thought he was spying on them".

Second man: "Ooooh, yes".

Me: "Yes, you know, that mutual English-Welsh suspicion. I was reading that bit last night. But I stopped to talk to you because this is my fifth day's walking now".

First man: "Is It?"

Me: " Yes, and in all that time I've only seen two other people standing by the roadside talking....and that was two ladies at the other side of Bala.

Second man: "Ha, ha, ha, haaa".

Me: "Now, Borrow's book is full of accounts of where he sees people by the side of the road and he stops to talk to them".

First man: "There you are, then".

Me: "But it seems that people don't do that any longer".

First man: "No, no, they don't."

Me: "So I was pleased to see you two here on a Sunday morning having a chat and enjoying the view".

Second man: "What part are you from?"

Me: "I live in Hereford".

Second man: " Oh, you live in Hereford".

First man: "You don't see, and nowadays even in this area, you ask somebody for directions and, see as children we knew where everywhere was, you know, the whole area, and erm, nowadays, ooh, I've only lived here about five year, I've got no idea, they have no interest at all where......."

Me: "....where places are, where people are, where people live".

First man: "I've got new neighbours now, well the first house they've been there two or three years, I'm sure now if I ask them what do you call that farm or that farm, or the one up there ....they would have no idea......"

Me: "No idea, no".

First man: "They've got no...."

Me: " No curiosity, no interest".

First man: "The caravan site here, my sister-in-law lives there, and er, the oil lorry wanted to deliver oil to Gyfaenog........."

Second man: "Oh, yes".

First man: "....... which is up by the old quarries, there's old quarries that's what the industry....."

Me: "Yes, I read the information board in the village. It mentions the quarries".

First man: ".....and, er, course she was brought up in that farm when she was a child, she says: "Well, really, I can't direct you now because there was the new forestry roads", and she didn't know if the old tramway, the tramway went to the quarry but it's been made into a road now, it was suitable for a lorry with a load of oil, you see. She says, " I'll tell you what, I'll come up with you, she says",".

Me: "Did she?"

First man: "And she went up in the oil lorry with the driver, it's not an easy place to direct anybody now"

Me: "There's hospitality for you".

First man: "But you don't find people, they're not around to...".

Me: "No, no, nobody's out and about, they're either indoors watching TV or they're driving along in their cars".

Second man: "Hee, hee, hee".

Me: "People don't do sociable standing around and chatting any longer".

Second man: "Oh, no".

Me: "I've asked various people, I've been inquisitive as I've gone along, I've asked people where places are or how old buildings are but nobody seems to know anything any longer".

First man: "Where do you make for now. You going into Cemmaes village?"

Me: "No, I'm not. I don't have the energy for detours, but I'm heading for Machynlleth now".

Second man: "You're going to carry on this back road, then?"

Me: "I am".

First man: "This won't take, you'll see Cemmaes, there's a bailey bridge, a steel bridge going to Cemmaes off this road, er, in about two and a half miles.

Second man: "What about after Machynlleth? Over to Llanidloes?"

Me: "After Machynlleth George Borrow went to Ponterwyd."

First man: "Yes, before you go into town, into the village. Isn't it, the George Borrow Hotel in Ponterwyd?"

Me: "I shall have to make sure I stay there then".

First man: "You've got a good walk to do then."

Me: "Yes, I've miles to go before I sleep."

Second man: "Ohh, yes".

Me: "I've done five days which is enough at once. I shall probably go home to rest my feet. But finish it I will, for I've just had my sixtieth birthday and it's now or never!"

First man: "Post Office Telephones, I worked for. It was interesting going, you know, even now, y'know, if you said to me I'm looking for a house so and so if they were on the telephone when I came to by there........ I maintained the telephones in this area for about 27 years in this com here cos I worked in Ponterwyd like where George Borrow Hotel is..."

Second man: "Yes, yes".

First man: "......and I knew all the places"

Me: "You got to know the area very well?"

First man: "I did, yes. In Wales."

Second man: "Aah, yes"

First man: "Yeah, and this morning now the, erm, the prime minister have said, erm....needs translate isn't it.....could you have a discussion on abortion again in Parliament, it's on the news this morning, and then there was a man, er, a specialist with abortion, and with premature child babies from the hospital in near Rhyll, that's right in north Wales, erm, discussing this"

Me: "Do you consider Welsh your mother tongue, then? Do you think in Welsh? You were translating just then?"

First man: "Yes, there are certain words, we tend to use the English word, er, especially with new things such as abortion."

Me: "Where there's no Welsh equivalent"

First man: "There's a lot of English words in our Welsh, innit?"

Second man: "Oh, arr".

First man: "But we're not very particular, erm, the Welsh people now that have been brought up they were, you see, for instance I used to help with the Eisteddfod on the stage and I've always said stage, y'see, but the Welsh word for it is (unintelligible), the youngsters today, they wouldn't say stage, they'd say (unintelligible), you see..."

Second man: " Argh, yes"

First man: "......they speak better Welsh than us, but I used to say I speak Welsh but not I was brought up, but, y'see, in, I went to the village school here, you passed it just beyond that, er, that, you had to speak English there, you had to put your hand up, please miss, can I go out to the toilet, see, please can I go......... and actually when I was a child here, there was one English family here and I lived in the farm the other side of the village, just below the village hall there and we used to sell retail milk in the village and before going to school in the morning we used to deliver milk to the top of the village, and the milk at night was delivered to the bottom part of the village, y'see".

Second man: "Ohhh, yerse:

First man: " And I remember going to Mr Russell's house at the top and there was some notice on the gate and I was delivering milk so I could've been nine or ten cos I went to the grammar school at eleven."

Second man: "Eleven, yeh."

First man: "And there was a notice on the gate and I couldn't understand what it meant, and Olwen Gwynn, who was older than me, she came past and she says, "Please use other gate". They were trying to tell people to go to the back door instead of where we used to go, and I couldn't read it and, when I was sixteen I had to work, to go to work to Birmingham and I hadn't, er, I could read English, I could write English but to converse in English I had no experience of it."

Me *(by now stunned into speechlessness)*:"Um. Urm."

First man: "I had, I learnt a lot from Peter the little boy of the English people Gwynon Davies......"

Second man: "Ohhhm yess."

First man: "....who used to come to the farm, he was too young to go and they were English people, they were second class compared with us, they were above us and they demanded that we delivered the milk before eight in the morning and we'd rush to get there. So my mother said to David my younger brother, "Take Peter home", so she heard him going along the yard, telling all of this, you came down yourself and we in Welsh tend to say and yes the translation for it, yes, well you go home yourself."

Second man: "Ha, ha, ha, ha."

First man: "I found when I went to work to Birmingham, I found it quite difficult to converse in Welsh to express yourself in Welsh although I could read it and write it, but no....."

Second man: "Read and write, ohh yess."

First man: "....but there's so much English come in, there were the only two people in the village."

Me (at last): "What year was that, you were referring to?"

First man: "Well, erm, just pre-war, just before the war broke out."

Me: "Ah, I see."

First man: "And somebody was on the Welsh now, giving,er, history on (unintelligible), y'know, and he was saying about being called up in July 1939 and he was in the army when he heard, erm, Neville Chamberlain coming back from Munich saying I've got a piece of paper here and then, a few days after, we are at war with Germany, I remember hearing it."

Me: "A serious moment."

First man: "That was, erm, cos I went to the grammar school in 39 so that was about 37, 38, yup."

Me (desperate): "Thank you. That's very interesting local history. I'm sorry to have taken your time."

Second man: "Nooo, argggh, yes."

Me: "Thank you for stopping and talking at me. I must push on or I shall run out of steam. Diolch yn fawr."

After this lengthy exchange, I reeled away down the lane, stunned by the man's garbled and garrulous speech. This, rather one-sided conversation was not as interesting as most of those that Borrow recounted although it had revealed some snippets of local history. Neither of the two men or me could converse about Welsh bards or legends and I had found it difficult to make any meaningful contribution. It is an interesting testimony to man's inability to express himself clearly and without hesitation and deviation, perhaps aggravated by being partly bi-lingual. I'd had my tape recorder running from start to finish.

At a quarter past eleven I noticed twelve wind turbines, whose blades only were visible, just over the ridge-line of Mynydd y Cemmaes, and they were slowly rotating in the soothing and gentle way they have, at a speed that never seemed to change, regardless of the force of the wind. Beguiling and bewitching I thought they were for there was no wind at all in the Dovey Valley that morning, I can't accept that having those softly revolving blades, those entirely benign machines, just discernible behind the hill, well camouflaged against the silvery sky, is an undesirable intrusion on the landscape. As we must have some alternatives to burning fossil fuels, some amenity sacrifices must be made and we must start somewhere with the process of getting our power from sustainable sources.

As I passed the road junction where the lane leads across the Dovey to Cemmaes village I thought again of Borrow's extraordinary account of his experience at the inn there. There'd been no traffic on the road at all since leaving Aberangell, except for three cyclists. At home, on a Sunday, the roads seem no quieter than during the week! I spied a pair of redstarts, quite a rarity in this terrain, a scattering of swallows swooping and twirling amongst the insects over the road, a pair of chaffinches and a pied wagtail sitting on the telephone wires, two crows and a poor rabbit, obviously incapacitated by myxomatosis, cowering by the verge.

At twelve-twenty I came to the B4404 where there appeared to be no route choice - I would have to follow this road as far as Machynlleth. Oh, dear. More road, more tarmac, more traffic. Although there was a wide river plain here, there were no footpaths leading along it, so the road it would have to be. There was a wide verge to walk on, at least. Guns were firing up the hill to the right; target shooting on a Sunday for I could soon see a sandy patch and some targets on the hillside; the Dovey Valley Shooting Club. The road was at river level, so I had no view of the river and the hills on either side were planing down, becoming lower and less impressive and with grazing land stretching up to the ridges.

Borrow's narrative of his journey between Mallwyd and Machynlleth is rather sparse. After the pub incident at Cemmaes, he met a deaf man, encountered a funeral, spoke to a woman from Shropshire about the Welsh local people, spoke briefly to a roadman, and arrived at the Wynnstay Arms in Machynlleth at 5pm.

Just before one o'clock I came to Llanwrin. On the left at the start of the village was a group of six semi-detached council houses outside which two youths, wearing baseball caps back-to-front, were lovingly polishing an ancient Ford Escort. The old village proper was a mix of whitewashed and rendered bungalows and houses of varying ages, and a stone-built church, the peace of which was rumpled by the roaring of a digger excavating a track in the trees at the back of the village.

A former chapel, built in 1825, had been converted into what was possibly residential accommodation and boasted nine solar panels on the roof. On the pretty little village green a man made of straw and wearing sunglasses was sitting on the seat. At the end of the settlement a charming, whitewashed, neat little cottage set in a garden at the edge of a wood was almost submerged in a frothy tide of hanging baskets containing cascades of multi-coloured nasturtiums. Satellite dishes were abundant here, possibly due to poor terrestrial TV reception.

The vast, flat river-plain meadows beyond the village had been cut for silage and now were cluttered with row upon row of black-plastic-covered silage rolls, gleaming in the sunlight. What a hideous example of visual pollution these black silage bales are; why can't the plastic be green and matt? Further on the fields had been cut, and cleared of hay, round their perimeters only, leaving standing grass in the centre. What could be the purpose of this? Then the rural silence was destroyed by the horrific racket of four tractors working in a team cutting hay in the final fields before the river curved in to meet the road thereby ending this long strip of fertile alluvial plain.

At Glan Fechan an elegant stone bridge rose over the river adjacent to a clear and shallow pool where fish were dimpling the surface of the water. At Pen y Bont I crossed the Dovey for the last time on yet another fine, ancient stone bridge. The river now was fully mature, fifty metres wide, clear, shallow and placid, easing its way along the terrain with very little fall and not quite yet subject to tidal rise and fall. I paused to enjoy, notwithstanding the bludgeoning traffic, the serene stream and pondered on the soothing and hypnotic effects of rivers and lakes, wherever they may be and regardless of the immediate surroundings.

I entered Machynlleth past the station, where trains were running on a Sunday, albeit not very frequently. The town is attractive, not having been ruined to any great extent by modern development in the town centre or even on the outskirts.

Standing on the lowest crossing point of the Dovey River, the town has its origins in pre-Roman times. The Romans built a military post at this strategic spot. In mediaeval times the town was an administrative centre for a very wide area and a focal point for trade, commerce and justice. In 1402 Owain Glyndwr was crowned King of Wales in the main street Heol Maengwyn. It still has an indefinable period atmosphere which sits rather uneasily with the constant surge of traffic. There is an impressive, neo-gothic town clock at the main road junction which was built in 1878 - so Borrow wouldn't have seen it - to commemorate the coming of age of Viscount Castlereagh, the fifth son of the Marquis of Londonderry. The most imposing building in the town is Plas Machynlleth which, along with its grounds, was given to the town in 1947 by the seventh Marquis of Londonderry, the great-grandson of Sir John Edwards who had the house built between 1780 and 1850.There is a fine modern memorial to Owain Glyndwr in front of the mansion which itself is now used as a museum of Celtic heritage.

There are seven pubs in Machynlleth and the famous Centre for Alternative Technology which is a little way out of town. The local authority has been busy setting-up a network of cycling trails from the town which are carefully and neatly signposted. Borrow mentions at some length the Glyndwr crowning, the poet Iolo Goch who greeted Glyndwr with a poem, the would-be assassin Dafydd Gam, who did not succeed in killing Glyndwr, and the bard Lawdden.

I found the pink-painted bed and breakfast house at the far end of town without any difficulty.

The Penrhos Arms, Cemmaes

The entrance to Plas Machynlleth

The Wynnstay Arms at Machynlleth

Owain Glyndwr's Senate House at Machynlleth

OVER THE HILLS AND FAR AWAY

The route that Borrow took from Machynlleth to Ponterwyd is difficult to establish with any precision from his text. Leaving Machynlleth he "ascended a steep hill" and walked "up and down" through scenery that was "beautiful to a degree with lofty hills on either side clothed most luxuriantly with trees of various kinds, but principally oaks." He was obviously not at his descriptive best that day.

He asked the way of " an old man working with a spade in a field near a gate" and spoke with him of the Bible and Twm o'r Nant. Name places were in short supply for Borrow on that day's walk but he did talk to numerous people on his way. He passed a house called Waen y Bwlch and in due course came to Esgyrn Hirion, neither of which can I find on a modern map. At the latter place he passed some sociable time in the office of the Potosi Mining Company, where lead was being mined not far from Plynlimon, and later came to a cottage Called Gwen Frwd where no-one spoke English. He saw a mountain called "Gaverse", which I cannot identify, and duly arrived at Ponterwyd.

From Machynlleth to Plynlimon one can either take the valley road as far as Talbontdrain and then forest tracks to reach the plateau to the west of the mountain or one can head out onto open ground and follow footpaths and bridlepaths. It is not clear which route Borrow took: there are clues in his text that suggest either route. Along the western side of Plynlimmon there is nowadays really no route choice as the Nant y Moch reservoir bars the way but this was doubtless not in existence when Borrow passed by.

Because I had walked the open ground route on a previous occasion, and because it was raining when I set off from Machynlleth and the clouds were low, I decided to take the valley road. This led pleasantly, after the council houses, through a golf course and some common land to the village of Forge which was a pretty cluster of cottages amongst the trees by the river; the stone-built chapel was dated 1862. Borrow refers in his book, continually, to a "road", and "a good road", which it is difficult to establish the meaning of 150 years later.. Forestry had been clear-felled on the right hand hillside where natural regeneration was taking place with scrub and young trees, both coniferous and deciduous, re-populating the steep slope. The lane was a delight to walk on: no traffic; uncut hedges on both sides full of butterflies and bird life, oak and ash and elder and hazel, hawthorn, wild roses, and much abundance of wild flowers. No-one to talk to except a small boy on a bike, no-one about on foot, no-one in evidence round the dwellings.

Coniferous plantations, very regimented, clothed the upper hillsides which would have been bare in the 1850s, but the lower slopes near the valley floor were thick with mature oak and ash woodland which mostly looked to be more than 150 years old. Nevertheless it was a very attractive landscape; wooded interlocking spurs gave the valley an air of mystery, so I reached each turn with anticipation to see how the view would change. Small, intimate hills rolled out the undulations of the skylines; it was very peaceful and quiet. The hills began to increase in height as I proceeded up the valley, walking next to the stream which ran clear and cool and pure through the hazel and alder trees along the banks. The higher ramparts of Plynlimon were clear of cloud, rising high against the grey ahead. I passed a converted chapel and adjacent dwelling, apparently now a holiday home for it was deserted, but which had its own public phone box and post box.

At Talbontdrain the old farm had become a guest house and hill-walking centre. It was an attractive white washed farmhouse, facing south, on Glyndwr's Way. At northings 954 my map showed that the tarmac road ended but I found that it continued straight ahead. This could of course have been the spot where Borrow "passed through a deep dingle and shortly afterwards came to the termination of the road". Here he "bore away to the right making for the distant mountain."

The road now descended to the river in the valley bottom, the Afon Hengwm, where the tarmac did finally end and I swung right (as indeed Borrow had done) onto a well-maintained forest track through a newish coniferous plantation mixed with some ash and oak. I came to a footbridge over the stream Nant Taren-Fedw-Ddu which I found entirely by chance as it was hidden by bushes beyond which the path led into an open area of gorse bushes where I was considerably scratched. This gave way to a huge open meadow thickly populated with thistles and sheep. By ten o'clock I had reached the top corner of this field and re-entered coniferous forest where the gradient suddenly increased alarmingly so it was hard sweating for half an hour through the drab and dingy closeness of the young spruce trees. The whole sweep of the opposite steep hillside was blanketed in conifers, in a dark green mat, depressingly dense and uniform, an alien form of vegetation slapped down on a dramatic landscape of deepening valley and high steep hillside. The monotony was broken by some patches of clear felling which had left brown, messy scars, and some natural streaks of scree, grey and matt, sharply contrasting the spiky conifer green.

I'd hoped to enjoy the spectacle of the cliff of Creigiau Bwlch Hyddgen but this was no rocky crag as shown on the map, but merely a precipitous stretch of shale and grass near the skyline, so in that respect the map was misleading.

The path eventually levelled out and so I paused to wipe sweat from my head and face at the point where my passage was blocked by a mammoth, tracked forestry machine that straddled the path. This monster had a jib with a huge pulley wheel carrying a cable for, I presumed, towing felled trees down, or up, the slopes on either side of the path. The operator had got his cable in a tangle and was evidently not in a good mood, for when I said, brightly " Hello, how're you doing, not a bad morning, plenty of work here, then", he replied not one word. Just beyond this mechanical and human disaster, were two more machines, one loaded with tree trunks ready to be shipped out of the forest and the other, the like of which I'd never seen, had a fearsome arrangement of serrated cutting wheels and seemed to be used for stripping branches, twigs and bark from the felled trunks. The whole area, left and right, had been clear felled but, bizarrely, three tall, branchless trunks had been left in splendid isolation amid the chaos of stumps, brashings and unwanted boles. Neat piles of branchless trunks, remarkably free of irregularities and about five metres long, obstructed the forest track. The whole forest to my left, on the lower slopes of Llechwed Diflas had been clear-felled and looked utterly desolate, destroyed, mangled, dead, tragic.

> *"O, if we but knew what we do*
> *when we delve or hew-*
> *hack and rack the growing green"*
> (Gerard Manly Hopkins' 'Binsey Poplars')

I came to the point shown on the map as a corner of the forest where the footpath and bridlepath diverged. However, my map was chronically out of date for the land ahead, shown as open land , was now forested, and the land on the left, shown forested, had been clear-felled. Unexpectedly the forest road now became, for a short stretch, a tarmac surface, and frequent signs informed me that this was the Mach3 cycle route, one of those that I'd read about in Machynlleth. The otherwise smooth contours of the ridge to the east were interrupted by two distinct man-made features: the twin pimples of cairns right on the skyline . There were several of these shown on the map thereabouts but the complexity of the topography and the difficulty of working out intervisibility meant that I could not decide where they were exactly.

By ten thirty-five I did finally come to the end of the forest and faced out across an immense expanse of high moorland in a wide shallow U, sweeping from the Plynlimmon ridges to the east across to Bryn Moel to the west. A very sudden change from the muggy claustrophobia of the spruce forest to this huge airy landscape in khaki and purple, a dramatic lengthening of the vista from twenty metres to twenty kilometres. Behind me the trees were hissing and whistling at me in the rising wind but in front the high moors were silent.....except for the ugly roar of a petrol strimmer. What on earth was going on? Well, as far as I could see someone was strimming the open hillside. Strewth, were they short of work to give the bloke? A huge sense of space and freedom beset me as I entered this panorama of brown hills overshadowed by the massive purple, hazy bulk of Plynlimon. As I crossed the bridge over the Llygnant stream I passed a digger dredging the stream by the bridge and I realised then that the strimming must be part of a stream clearance project.

There were sheep pens and barns at Hyddgen. I was hoping to see some sign of former mining buildings which could have been the Potosi Mine at which Borrow received some hospitality but Hyddgen was evidently not it. Borrow was told by a young man at the mine that the Potosi Mining Company was the richest in all Wales. The original Potosi Mines were in Peru and **they** were the richest in South America. The stony track led ahead. winding across the contours of this upland wilderness where an awe-inspiring range of country was visible. There were few sheep on this desolate and deserted moor but the hand of man is never out of sight for very long because soon the waters of Nant y Moch reservoir came into sight as a thin crescent of grey water, astonishingly flat and level in this landscape of hills, curves and contours. It was also an intrusion of a different colour into the dun and ochre of the surrounding hills.

At eleven forty-five I came to the river crossing over the Afon Hengwm (not the same river as I'd encountered earlier, but it's odd to find two rivers with the same name so close together) which was a considerable torrent and I was dismayed to find no bridge but merely a ford, which I would not be able to negotiate dry-shod. I cast around a bit, thinking that there must be a bridge somewhere, and, sure enough, found a rusty old footbridge a little way upstream. Borrow didn't mention any difficulty crossing watercourses nor did he comment on the sizeable sheep population. Just beyond, I passed some ruined stone walls and the remains of a building, possibly a relic of summer sheep herding. (Not the Potosi mine, either). I could now see down the wide flat strath of the eastern arm of the reservoir, an opening which increased the air of space and light in this already vast open space.

The expanding view of the reservoir and its seductively curvaceous shoreline introduced a new element into the vertical curves of the hills. I could see a lone four-square building on a promontory on the northern side of the reservoir's north-west arm which I took to be the remains of the mining buildings at Llechwedd Mawr. (Possibly Potosi). One solitary tree mirrored this single man-made object, standing against the unvegetated hillside. The incessant wind stroked the grasses and reeds in the boggy ground like a hairbrush; the lake expanded as I walked providing a dead flat plane, a level and even valley floor as it were, and whose banks fitted exactly the contours of the hills in which it sat.

At Maesnant I passed the first habitable house that I'd seen since Talbontdrain , though it was actually deserted. There were also two barns here, presumably for the sheep business. However, the sign on the gate stated that this was "Maesnant Outdoor Pursuits Centre", so it was not connected any longer with farming. Here the stony track finally became tarmac which was to last until Ponterwyd. A line of telephone poles now followed the road, so Maesnant, isolated though it was, had a phone connection. I passed a green and fertile gully, in which the Maesnant stream tumbled down some falls, creating spray and giving life to a dense thicket of bush, scrub and trees in the defile.

Across the lake the hill Drosgol was a stark, bare, unadorned humpback of a hill, an unbroken sweep of brown hillside, almost symmetrical, dominating the view. I passed a single car parked at the side of the road, no-one in it and no-one in sight. The far end of the reservoir was sharply defined by the dense green of the coniferous forest on the hillside beyond, but the forested area was shown as open land on my map and the forested area on the map had been felled. This, once again, showed how quickly the work of man could invalidate a map but using an old map at least had the effect of concentrating the mind on the landscape!

Crossing the Nant y Moch stream, by a bridge, I passed a water pumping station. and paused to admire the staggered line of the stream as it fell down the long hillside from the Plynlimon ridge far above. The whole length of this level ridge, notchy, distant, hazy and purple against the silvery sky, could be seen from this viewpoint . A planning notice on a pole informed passers-by that Airwave MM02 was applying to Ceredigion Council for permission to install two co-linear antennae, and equipment ancillary thereto, at Nant y Moch Pumping Station. Huh, more jargon and more mobile phone masts, I supposed, but where were all the potential users in this deserted landscape? And what did the wind-turbine objectors have to say about these damn things springing up in their ugly metallic forms across the country? Not much, I imagine, for I suspect that they use mobile phones themselves for trivial chitchat and unnecessary calls whereas a wind-turbine, oh no, they have no direct personal use for that and it won't help them manage their hectic daily schedule of work, shopping and text messages.

The terrain was gaunt, raw, wild and remote and vastly refreshing but man had put his careless hand on the land again and dumped a microwave oven just beyond the pumping station. The water pipe from the latter was buried by the track and visible only by virtue of a line of manhole covers and small, carefully-built stone abutments where the pipe crossed over streams coming down the hillside. At the last stream crossing a track led down to the waterside, with a gated entrance and sign which stated that the property was private, that permit holders only were allowed, that bathing was forbidden and dogs must be kept under control. More dog-in-the-manger, then.

I paused for a rest, when I came to the public road at around one o'clock, in the lee of yet more conifer trees. Inspecting my map, I was dismayed to find that the hotel at which I was booked for the night, the Dyffryn Castell, was not at Ponterwyd but about two miles to the east on the A44 trunk road. Oh, dear, what bad news; another dangerous and poisonous trudge on a main road. At spot height 396 (over 1200 feet) I had a spectacular view of the reservoir dam which formed an unnaturally abrupt end to the crescent of water. This massive wedge of hard-edged, angular masonry sat uneasily in the softness of its wild surroundings. The dam wall itself looked too thin and feeble to hold back the enormous weight of water in the reservoir, even though it was supported by huge triangular buttresses. The far side of the dam structure continued as an overflow cascade which stepped down to the stream bed far below where the dam outflow meandered through some fairly rocky and steep terrain. The forestry planting on the far hillside had been carried out with some sensitivity for it was not straight-lined or solid but the trees had a scattered and more natural appearance.

The first building I came to was a working farm with bales of hay in the barns and a brand new pick-up attached to a horse box. Over to the west an iron-age hill fort was visible, with a more modern structure adjacent which, the map indicated, was a ventilation shaft, though why it was there I couldn't imagine...unless that was the Potosi mine. The farm at Aber Peithnant was also a working farm close to which a footbridge led over the river on the line of the bridleway. The river valley, up which I could see at this point, was deep in a rocky gorge, and resembled the Eyrieux valley in the Ardeche: wild, remote, rugged, unspoilt and made perfect by a waterfall tumbling down to it from the hillside behind.

The ancient cairns and stone circle at Y Garnedd were only discernible in the form of one low, flat-topped hillock which was doubtless an eroded and diminished burial chamber. Similarly, Carn Llwyd was barely visible as an ancient tumulus, merely a small spur on the hillside with a ditch on the uphill side. Hirnant was a pretty farm house set in a wooded dingle shortly beyond which the waters of Dinas Reservoir came into sight. Two alien objects in the landscape were water company pump houses, clearly visible on the shores of the reservoir. Another unpleasant man-made item was the conifer plantation on Banc Creignant Mawr which was a truly dense, unremitting congestion of dark green.

I finally put the umbrella away and three minutes later it began to rain again. I came to the Dinas Reservoir car park where an information board, supplied by E-On, stated: *"These two reservoirs are part of PowerGen's hydro power station which generates enough power to supply Aberystwyth and the surrounding area with clean, environmentally-friendly electricity for most of the year. The Dinas reservoir is stocked with brown and rainbow trout"*. This boast of green-ness was a little diminished by the sight of a litter bin overflowing with plastic trash more of which was blowing around the car park in the breeze and sticking to the fencing.

The next dwelling, a sheep farm, featured a large kids' trampoline in the garden and about sixty sheep penned in an area grazed down to the mud, so they were effectively without food. Bounce the kids, but don't feed the sheep. Another planning application notice, dated May 2001, pinned to a telephone pole, where it had evidently been for over three years, was for overhead power cables from the Cefn Groes Windfarm to the network substation at Rhydlyddan, with a map showing the proposed line of the cables. I peered more closely at the map on the pole, hmm, seems to cover this area, so the cable will be......about over there. I turned to look over my shoulder and, sure enough, there marching over the hill Drybedd was a line of new posts and cable. So planning consent was granted and the system is up and running. Well, it seemed that windpower was going ahead round here, despite the usual NIMBY moaning and objections, and being distributed by new overhead cables. How reassuring.

From the high point of the road beyond the reservoir I looked down on to Ponterwyd, an attractive grouping of apparently three separate communities of white-painted houses set amongst the trees looking pretty and innocuous in the rural landscape, even though I know that the A44 roared through it. I wouldn't have to go into the village so I took a footpath shortcut to the A44....and promptly wished I hadn't for the ground was an appalling quagmire of tussock and deep muddy holes, all steeped in water. A lengthy struggle with this rebarbative muck brought me to the A44 at twenty past two. I made a short detour into Ponterwyd and found a tourist information board by the bridge in the village centre which read:

" *A community began to grow in the eighteenth century around the first bridge.The population rose as local lead mines expanded and the village grew to include a Methodist chapel, a school and an inn during the nineteenth century. The Bridge Fair was held annually in the village. Drovers came here to buy local cattle and sheep to sell at English markets, especially at Barnet, near London.*" (Me, I attended the Queen Elizabeth's Boys' Grammar School in Barnet from 1955 to 1962). " *By the early twentieth century most of the lead mines had closed but the area was becoming popular with visitors on motoring, cycling and walking tours. A garage opened in the village and also a youth hostel.*" (Which certainly isn't there now). " *The village was ahead of its time when the waters of the river were harnessed to produce electricity here in the 1930s. Erwyd Mill was converted from a corn mill into a hydro-electric power station and villagers paid one pound a year to have electric lighting in their homes. The mill has now gone but the old power house still stands alongside the bridge*".

After a brief rest to gird my loins for the gruesome tridge along the A44, I began the long toil to the hotel at Duffryn Castell which was around two miles east of Ponterwyd. The road was a noisy, dangerous, fume-filled trench and Wild Wales it suddenly was not. There was no footway; the trucks pounded past full of supermarket goods only inches from my left shoulder; the boy-man racers roared by in their four by fours; none slowed down for the vulnerable human on foot.

Although I was not aware of it at the time, the George Borrow Hotel does still exist in to the east of Ponterwyd on the A44 so that must have been where he put up for the night. Borrow went to Dyffryn Castell* to find a guide to take him to the top of Plynlimmon the day after he arrived at Devil's Bridge. He could, of course, have saved some walking if he'd tackled the mountain from Ponterwyd, but perhaps he thought that Devil's Bridge was closer to the mountain than Ponterwyd, due to his lack of maps . His guide on his ascent was in fact the innkeeper, a man who "had much more the appearance of a native of Tipperary than a Welshman." *(How does a Welshman look different from an Irishman, George?)*. Borrow asked the man why it was called Duffryn Castell and the reply was that there used to be a castle in the valley opposite the inn which also gave its name to the river in the valley, the Afon Castell. Borrow could see no sign of the remains of a castle and nor could I when I looked for it the next morning.

I finally arrived at the hotel, considerably battered in spirit, at three o'clock and much in need of beer. It was an unimpressive roadside inn, right on the main road, with a rather worn and tired appearance inside and out. But I got my beer and then lay down for a couple of hours before returning to the bar. At seven fifteen there were three Irishmen, four Russians and four others of indeterminate nationality, all workers judging by their dirty clothes and all ordering food and drinking lager. By half-seven, the Irish had departed and been replaced by three Welshmen speaking English.

As far as I could tell from the talk that I could understand, they were all working on the new overhead power cables. Whilst waiting for my food, I looked out of the window to see thirteen cars in the car park and three vans labelled GE Wind Energy, so that was definitely it. Having eaten, I went outside to sit in front of the hotel to enjoy the summer evening. I sat with my feet virtually in the road - the main road to Aberystwyth , for that's all the room there was, and withdrew them every time a juggernaut hove into view. The green hills over the way were hued pink by the evening sun; between the traffic I could hear the bleating of sheep and the chirping of sparrows. A bunch of swallows wheeled round a mobile phone mast on the hillside in a grove of trees; it was a warm and balmy evening and anywhere away from the road it would have been idyllic.

***

Most place names in Wales are compound names consisting of several separate nouns and adjectives that describe the geographical location. They often look incomprehensible but if broken down into their constituent parts they do make sense.

For example, Pontrhydygroes can be written Pont-rhyd-y-groes. Where 'pont' is 'bridge', 'rhyd' is 'ford', 'y' is 'the' and 'groes' is 'cross', the name means 'The bridge of the ford of the cross'. A bit of mental juggling is needed to get at the sense of this but, presumably, there's a river which used to crossed by a ford where a bridge was subsequently built and all situated where there was, or still is, a cross (probably originally a preaching cross).

Others are harder to fathom. Pen Drws y Coed literally translated means 'The top of the gap in the wood' which may have been geographically accurate at the time when it was named.

Pont Aberglaslyn, or Pont-aber-glas-llyn, literally translated would mean 'The bridge of the mouth of the grey lake'.

Aberystwyth means 'The mouth of the River Ystwyth'

Eighth day

HISTORICAL DIVERSIONS

Borrow reached his accommodation at Ponterwyd, coming from the north, without descending to the river and so I had assumed that the inn at which he stayed was to the north-west of the main village. However, the information board in the village states that he did stay at the inn that now bears his name which actually sits on the main road a short way west of the settlement. His text details a long and rather confrontational conversation that he had with the landlord and with two others who were in the kitchen at the time. He found a walking companion on his route to Devil's Bridge the next day with whom he conversed on a variety of subjects until they arrived at Ysbytty Cynfyn. Borrow arrived at Devil's Bridge mid-morning. He stayed at an inn that he called a 'hospice' and which he did not name but described as "an immense lofty cottage with projecting eaves and a fine window to the east which enlightens a stately staircase and a noble gallery. It fronts the north and stands in the midst of one of the most remarkable localities in the world, of which it would require a far more vigorous pen than mine to convey an adequate idea". He made an excursion to the summit of Plynlimon the next day, November 5th, with a guide, the innkeeper at Duffryn Castell.

The following day he went to Hafod Ychdryd, by a route too inadequately described to follow, then to Pont y Groes , Spytty Ystwyth, Fair Rhos, Pont Rhyd Fendigaid, Strata Florida and passed the night at the Talbot Arms at Tregaron. My route, then, would be, for the most part, clearly defined.

As I was putting vaseline on my feet in the lobby of the Duffryn Castell Hotel* prior to my departure a bearded walker, draped in waterproof clothing and carrying a huge rucksack, arrived and muttered:

"Are you staff or a guest? Is the hotel open? I want to ask them for some breakfast"

I said, "Yeah, why not? Breakfast doesn't finish until nine."

Before I'd got my boots on he reappeared, muttered "Oh, I suppose it was too much to expect" and went out of the door. A couple of minutes later I saw him climbing over a stile and heading up the hillside into the drizzle. The cloud base was at about 1200 feet so most of the hill tops were cloaked in hill-fog and mist wreathed the valleys. It was damp and dismal, but not so wet that I had to erect the umbrella.

Very soon after leaving the hotel I was able to escape the purgatory of the A44 by taking the B4323 which was signposted to Devil's Bridge, or rather to Pont ar Fynach, or the Bridge on the River of the Monk. Of Borrow's two interlocutors in the inn at Ponterwyd, one said that it is called the Devil's Bridge because " 'tis said that the Devil built it in the old time", and the other said " I have heard that the Devil had no hand in the work at all, but that it was built by a Mynach or monk".

As I ambled along this quiet country road, in the grey drizzly mist, I appreciated that the presence of mist, or hill-fog, lends the hills an air of mystery, of magic, especially when the mist is gently moved along by the wind. One cannot tell how much of a hill is concealed; the clearings in the mist reveal hitherto hidden parts of the landscape; one's view is changing as one walks but also shifting with the windows in the mist. Mist also deadens sound; there was certainly little to be heard that morning. *"All the air a solemn stillness holds"* was the line from Gray's Elegy that repeated itself in my head.

The local drivers had a habit of saluting walkers, so I was waving back to those motorists who waved at me - I supposed it was a courteous acknowledgement of one's presence. Very civilised. It was an interesting and pleasing landscape, small scale but rugged with many changes of level, spurs coming down from the hills above, tumps and bumps in the valley, clumps of deciduous trees, heather and bracken and scree in pleasant juxtaposition on the hillsides.

Around nine o'clock I joined the A4120 at Tynyfordd, a literal translation of 'House on the Road', which seemed to have little traffic, to my relief because, as the grass in the fields was now sopping wet, I'd decided to stick to the roads, this morning at least. Lovely sheep-studded meadows led down to the River Rheidol which ran in a deepening gorge beyond which the open hillside of bracken and heather was cluttered with outcrops and boulders. All in perfect balance and harmony and, as such, very gratifying to gaze upon. *(Crikey, I'm starting to sound like Borrow)*

The church of St John the Baptist at Yspytty Cynfyn* was an unattractive rough-cast rendered, unadorned block. There was a rusty chain dangling externally to ring the single bell in the roof-belfry and, oddly, five monkey-puzzle trees in the churchyard. The earliest date I could find on the headstones was 1793. I had made a small detour to visit this church because the clergy used to arrive at it from the other side of the river by means of the famous Parson's Bridge which lies a short way down the hillside. Borrow had been urged to visit this bridge by his walking companion, but did not; nor did I.

I passed a scruffy caravan site at Erwbarfe, a form of visual pollution that Borrow wouldn't have had to suffer and, shortly after, some meadows littered with black plastic silage bales. He wouldn't ever have seen any of those, either.

At nine thirty-five I came to Devil's Bridge, passed the tea-rooms, bulging with tourist knick-knackery but deserted, and entered a gloomy, leafy tunnel where the trees overhung the road and where the roar of waters told of the proximity of the waterfalls. On the bridge itself, there was a closed refreshment shop and, on both sides of the road, turnstiles operable by coin-in-the-slot to allow one access to the gorge walks. For £2.50 one could see the nature trail, the waterfalls, the three bridges, the monks route, Jacob's Ladder, the 100 steps and the Robber's Cave in half an hour. For £1, and in ten minutes, one could view the three bridges and the Devil's Punchbowl. Iron railings along the roadside prevented any access to these attractions other than through the turnstiles and I thought it disgraceful that visitors had to pay to view these natural features. In a greedy world I suppose that a landowner will always milk an opportunity for profit. I was rather depressed by this exploitation especially as Borrow had enjoyed these sights for free. There was no chance of scrambling down the neighbouring slopes either as high chain-link fences lined the road for some distance.

Borrow, however suffered no such impediments to a walk down into the gorge to view the falls and he waxes lyrically about this outing over three pages in his book.

The river was a very long way below the bridge where it rushed through a narrow, twisting rocky defile; through the overhanging luxuriant greenery where steps and handrails could be glimpsed. The sides of the gorge were very densely wooded with ash, oak and beech, loving the life in the damp air down there which also fed the abundant ferns and mosses on the trees and boulders. Unbidden, consciously at least, some lines from Wordsworth came into my head:

"The sounding cataract
haunted me like a passion: the tall rock,
the mountain, and the deep and gloomy wood,
their colours and their forms, were then to me
an appetite; a feeling and a love,
that had no need of a remoter charm."

The beauty of it all was compelling, to such an extent that I was tempted to put my money in the slot and do one of the walks. However, I found that I had no pound coins, so I moved on to the far end of the bridge to admire the Hafod Arms Hotel* which was, rather to my surprise, exactly as Borrow describes it. It was a very magnificent stone-built structure, with wide-projecting eaves supported on massive gallows brackets, a splendid Georgian-style arched window on the first floor (which he mentions), an annexe to the side with a turret on the roof, and with four storeys. A very untypical building, very idiosyncratic, most impressive. The scene was completed by the presence of an old-type AA phone box, No 289, in black with yellow trim and a pointed roof with four gables. The outbuildings, the walls to the carpark and gardens, the retaining walls were all stone-built, immaculate and very well-maintained.

There was little to be seen from the belvedere in front of the hotel but trees, lush rampant trees occupying the whole front view except.......through a small gap in the leafery I could make out a very deep valley beyond, where the Mynach and Rheidol rivers met, and on the gorge-side, far away, the thin silver thread of a waterfall. Mist was still creating mystery, wreathing the hilltops and ridges enclosing the gorges, drifting in and around the tree canopy.

Even though I was standing in front of the wonderful Hafod Arms, at that famous beauty spot Devil's Bridge on an August weekday, the place was deserted. There was no-one active or visible in or around the hotel, there was no-one enjoying the view or visiting the turnstile attractions and there was very little traffic on the road. I supposed that tourists went to Spain these days, not deepest Wales because there's not much kudos in that. Interestingly, Borrow, who passed three nights at the Hafod Arms,wrote: "The inn, of which I was the sole guest during the whole time that I continued there, has very few guests, except in summer, when it is thronged with tourists."

An information board just outside the railway station informed me that the name Mynach for the river recalls the close links between this place and the Cistercian Monastery at Strata Florida   (which, incidentally, is an Anglicised version of the Welsh name for the place, Ystrad Fflur, which actually translates as 'Valley of Flowers". It has nothing whatsoever to do with the USA or layers of rock!).The monastery owned huge estates in this part of Ceredigion. The Mynach flows through a narrow ravine before falling 100 metres in a series of cascades to join the Rheidol river in the Punchbowl.

The road bridge over the river is a triple structure where successive bridges have been built above the previous one. The first bridge was probably built by the monks in mediaeval times and in the early eighteenth century a second bridge was built above the first.This was strengthened and an iron balustrade was added in 1814. The present road bridge was added in the early twentieth century. Remarkably the two earlier bridges still survive, sheltered beneath the modern one (and are not visible when one is on it). Devil's Bridge has been a popular tourist attraction for over 200 years and was formerly part of the Hafod Estate, hence the name of the hotel. (More on Hafod later). Thomas Johnes, owner of Hafod from 1780 to 1816, developed the estate as a place of picturesqe splendour with dramatic walks, a model farm and extensive new plantations on the surrounding hills. In 1792 Johnes built a cottage-style inn to accommodate the visitors who came to admire the grand scenery. It soon became too small and, in 1814, he erected the present Hafod Arms to replace it. The top floor with Alpine roof and dormers was added in 1839 by the next owner of Hafod, the fourth Duke of Newcastle. In the 1820s a lead smelting works was built 500 metres west of the bridge. In 1902 the Vale of Rheidol railway was built to carry ore from the mines and timber from Hafod to the port at Aberystwyth.

Devil's Bridge station, at the terminus of the narrow-gauge Vale of Rheidol railway was also deserted. The platform area with two tracks and a crossover, the Portakabin cafe and the ticket office were devoid of life or activity.

By half-past ten I was still in Devil's Bridge for I had made the mistake of trying to cut out some road walking by use of a public footpath across some fields behind the shop opposite the station. This led me into a confusing morass of long, wet grass on rough tussocky ground and into an impenetrable tangle of felled woodland where the barrier of cut-off stumps, fallen branches, brashings and brambles made progress impossible. I had to return, now with wet feet, to the road at the shop and continue on tarmac. I then passed the post office and stores, which also provided bed and breakfast, where, unusually, three people were chatting over a cottage gate, but in English.

Of this village Borrow wrote: "It consists of only a few ruinous edifices, and is chiefly inhabited by miners and their families. I saw no men but plenty of women and children". I turned left at the post office onto the B4343 to Pontrhydygroes. Beyond the school, which marked the end of the village, the land was flatter, moory but with few ridges or distinct hills to lend character and interest to the terrain. I suspect that Borrow had not come this way but had taken the B4574 towards Cwmystwyth because he wrote: " The way lay up a hill to the south-east; on my way was a glen", *(only in Scotland, surely?)*, "down which the river of the Monk flowed with noise and foam". However, he evidently agreed with me about the terrain for he went on: "The country soon became naked and dreary, and continued so for some miles".

The road was without traffic; the clouds were still down on the hills behind me; the breeze brought a strong reminder that I was back in sheep country with a vengeance - that unique, acrid but sweet evocative odour of sheep dung. This was the Rhosygell where, bizarrely but thriftily, the farmer had capped his fence posts with car hub-caps, presumably collected from the roadside. Good recycling. The damp and misty air settling on the seeding grass heads in the fields adjacent to the road had turned the meadows into a sea of silver, a glimmering veil floating above the ground, a delicate filigree of water droplets and fine grass seeds.

Borrow's account of his walk this day made much of his visit to Hafod Ychdryd which he described as: "the summer mansion of Uchtryd which, from time immemorial, has been the name of a dwelling on the side of a hill above the Ystwyth, looking to the east. At first it was a summer boothie or hunting lodge to Welsh chieftains, but subsequently expanded into the roomy, comfortable dwelling of Welsh squires, where hospitality was much practised and bards and harpers liberally encouraged".
He devoted several pages of the book to Hafod and so I had decided that I must make the necessary detour to see what it was

like today. Accordingly, I took the shortest line that I could contrive from Devil's Bridge to Hafod (which was named as such on the OS map) by turning off the B4343 on a bridlepath which led south east. I was risking getting wet again from the knees downwards but it seemed worth the gamble. In the event the bridlepath was a track for half a kilometre and then the signs pointed off across open country, over a spur and valley terrain. The waymarking was inadequate and so the only way I could follow the correct line was by walking between the bridlepath gates - those with a tall handle on top of the gate which enabled a seated horse rider to open the gate. The area was, nevertheless, an attractive series of shallow cwms and ridges, intricate and quiet.

By eleven fifteen I reached the highest ridge on this path, at the corner of a conifer plantation to see ahead an upland wooded valley, with farm buildings and the forested Ystwyth valley beyond. Caermeirch, just before the B4574, used to be a sheep farm for it had all the necessary accessories: sheep pens, stone outbuildings, stone farmhouse but it was now empty, derelict and exuding an air of melancholy. Collapsed tin sheds, disused sheep feeders, sagging roofs bore the signs of long neglect.

I turned left and soon went right into the forest on the downhill slope towards the river, assuming that I was now on the Hafod estate. The woodland had been carelessly thinned leaving a clutter of felled trees, rotten logs and stumps, stripped branches and piles of twigs. Shortly I came to a dirt road below which, on the river flat, was a walled area containing some single storey buildings that looked, as far as I could see through the trees, to be in good order. It was as silent as the grave; there was no-one about and no signs of any recent activity. Was this the remains of Hafod? Was I trespassing? Who was it now owned by? Hmm. I examined the map and decided that the house of Hafod was further west than my present position so I turned right on the dirt road and ambled along through mature and diverse conifer woodland. At a track junction stood a sign bearing the legend "Estate Office". Hum, that smacks of Forestry

Commission. Rhododendrons, cypress and sycamore trees suggested a deliberate planting in the past rather than re-generation or forestry crop planting.

At the spot where the map suggested that the Hafod mansion* should be there was no sign of a mansion and all I could see through the trees was a huge plastic tunnel greenhouse and the roofs of some buildings tucked into the foot of the hillside. The trees were dense restricting visibility more than a little. I wandered out onto the open meadow of the river flat but could still see no mansion and because there was no-one about to ask and because I still didn't know if I was trespassing on a private estate I didn't dare go poking about too overtly. Disappointed, I returned to the woodland and continued west on the forest road along the hillside.

Borrow described the mansion as " a noble fairy place, beautiful but fantastic, in the building of which three styles of architecture seemed to have been employed. A gothic tower and an Indian pagoda at either end; the middle part had much the appearance of a Grecian villa". After gazing at "this house of eccentric taste for about quarter of an hour" Borrow followed the road in a "southerly" direction. *(Hah, wrong again, George, for the road following the river led west).* Presently he came to a gate, the boundary, in the direction in which he was going, of the Hafod domain.

Well, I followed the track through the trees and the silence: the only sound was the hissing and tinkling of the river Ystwyth to my left. Where the woodland ended I passed a sign inscribed "Forestry Commission", so that solved that conundrum. Sheep were grazing on the fertile, green river meadows. I walked on past a crag towering over the track and an ugly litter of derelict and rusting farm machinery, metal tanks and damaged feeder bins. The river, flowing shallow and clear, looked very inviting on this warm and muggy morning, as indeed do all these pure and sparkling Welsh streams. After what seemed to be an awfully long way, I too came to the gate. It was a fine, ornate piece of ironwork hung on elaborate stone pillars the effect of which was ruined by the obnoxious presence of a collection of rotting, rusting dumped cars at the track edge. Three huge and apparently aggressive labrador dogs came rushing at me from the adjacent gatehouse with a good deal of nasty barking and bared teeth. However, I escaped mauling by marching steadfastly ahead and hoping for the best.

A few metres beyond was the bridge of Pontrhydygroes* and a little cluster of stone cottages, one of which was a shop advertising hot drinks. A chance of some tea? The woman inside was already serving another customer so that slowed things down a bit, especially as there was evidently no hurry for anything hereabouts and it was some fifteen minutes later that I took my cup of tea outside to sit and enjoy the pleasant scene. What, I wondered, had changed since Borrow passed this way? Well, the bridge, the wooded slopes beyond the river, the cottages and the peace and quiet were all delightfully nineteenth century but the two defunct petrol pumps were decidedly not. The bridge itself was dated 1898 so was not the selfsame bridge that had born the weight of the peripatetic linguist from Norfolk.

I was joined at the tea-table by Mr Edwards, he of the shop, who regaled me for the best part of forty-five minutes with the history of the Hafod estate. He told me that I hadn't been able to find the house because it was no longer there. The mansion had been dynamited by the Forestry Commission in 1951 after his father had bought the house with a demolition order on it. The order had been made because the house had 365 windows (one for each day of the year: a rather more flamboyant architectural statement than the fifty-two windows of Sir Edmund Buckley) and so the house attracted a crippling sum in window taxes which no-one could afford to pay in the dog-days after WW2. A year or two later the local authority came to Hafod to enquire if it could use the house as a residential home only to find a pile of rubble.

Borrow comments that, whilst belonging to an ancient family of the name of Johnes, the house of Hafod was celebrated far and wide for its library containing, amongst other treasures, a collection of Welsh manuscripts. This famous library was destroyed in a fire that consumed the house. Borrow's literary and philological interests made him view the loss of the library as a far greater tragedy than the destruction of the house. Mr Edwards' memories, however, centred round the greed, arrogance and meanness that made up the iniquities of the squirearchy in the 1930s and 1940s. He was born and brought up on the estate, living under a pernicious feudal system that remained until the demise of the last squire of Hafod. He remembered his father refusing a gift of meat from the squire to help him feed his family of six on the grounds that he would not be patronised by accepting charity from such a man. He recounted the forelock tugging and bowing and scraping that occurred at the very gate through which I'd passed when the squire returned from Aberystwyth in his carriage. He spoke of how his father had installed the petrol pumps in the fifties to sell Russian petrol which caused milord to visit him in his cottage to say: " No-one makes a profit on this estate except for me". After a stand-up row, the squire caved in but on the condition that the petrol for sale was British and not Russian.

Well, that had all changed now. The mansion gone, the estate ruined by the Government, the woodlands in decay, the land leased to tenants who are not, unlike the Edwards family, in fief to an arrogant aristocracy.

In the village the Miner's Arms offered bed and breakfast but was closed for renovation. The Bethel Weslyan Chapel, dated 1874, was a handsome stone edifice, set in superior position above the village on the hillside towering over the public lavatories. This may have been where Borrow came across a wedding party and suffered ridicule by the locals on account of his non-local Welsh accent. The site where he saw "immense works of some kind in full play and activity, for engines were clanging and puffs of smoke were ascending from tall chimneys" was now a level plateau between the road and the river featuring a grimy car repair workshop, several bungalows and some ancient flat-roofed buildings which might have been part of the works that Borrow saw. He was told that it was called the Great Level, a mining establishment, and indeed there were still some piles of shaly waste material nearby. Along the road the houses were an uneasy mix of old stone houses and modern ugly bungalows.

From hereabouts Borrow reports: "Beyond the valley to the west was an enormous hill, on the top of which was a most singular-looking crag, seemingly leaning in the direction of the south". Well, I looked, and saw a disinctive sweep of scree, a dominant break in the densely wooded slopes of the Ystwyth valley, but leaning it was not.

In Ysbyty Ystwyth*, a pretty village of stone cottages, there were, remarkably, people to be seen. Three kids were sitting on a seat chewing gum, a young couple were walking their dog, which seemed virtually legless, a man in a top hat was leaning against a wall and three burly men were laying kerbstones. The chapel was dated 1836 and almost invisible in the immensely long grass *(why do we say 'long' grass and not 'tall' grass?)* of the neglected churchyard. Borrow described this village -whose name translates as 'Ystwyth Hospital" - by writing that "nothing but dirt and wretchedness were now visible".

He then entered upon a wild moory region, crossed a little bridge over a rivulet and seeing a small house on the shutter of which was painted "cwrw" (beer) he went in and ordered a pint of ale. He was told that the name of the rivulet was Afon Marchnand which led me to believe that the house was at Tanrhydiau, which was the closest building to the river shown on the map. My next waypoint was then the bridge over the Marchnant.

The terrain south of Ysbyty Ystwyth was soft and undulating but with no big ridges or hills. There were newish forestry plantations on the moor but the whole scene to the west was dominated by the gigantic rocky scar of the quarry on Graig y Bwlch. The hoppers, conveyors and buildings and the great pyramids of graded stone and the gaunt raw rock of the quarry face were an ugly intrusion into the soft pastoral landscape. The intrusion was made worse by the continual faint rattly-roar of stone crushers and the bright pinpoints of high-intensity light from five floodlights. The guts had been ripped out of the hill to create an appalling industrial blight.

I walked on through typical upland sheep-grazing land; boggy pastures with thistles, reeds and marsh grass; frequent streams trickling down the gentle hillside; scattered copses of hawthorn and ash; old hedgerows marked by lines of ancient trees. The bridge over the Marchnant was a modern structure for although the upper parts were stone the supporting beams were pre-cast concrete: no elegant self-supporting stone arches there! There were no buildings, or ruins, between the bridge and the farmstead of Tanrhydiau. As I approached this cluster of buildings on either side of the road I spied a woman leaving a barn to enter the house. I shouted to her: "Excuse me, do you live here?". She replied affirmitively and so I went on: "Did you know that the Englishman George Borrow stopped here in 1854, for this was an alehouse, to drink some beer?" She said, "Diw, Diw". I explained that Borrow had had his drink at what seemed to be the first house after the bridge and she agreed that it must have been here because there'd never been another house in the vicinity. I said that Borrow had walked from Caernarfon to Swansea, and I was following his route, to which she replied, "Diw, Diw". I asked:" I don't suppose you could give me a pint now, could you?", to which she responded: " Oh, indeed, no, we're all teetotallers here now, look. But thank you for telling us".

Borrow ordered his ale at this house in English, only to be told "Dim Saesneg" (I have no English). So he spoke to her in Welsh. Whilst drinking the home-made ale, Borrow complained:" Now there is something in this ale which ought not to be. It tastes very bitter. Is there no chwerwlys in it?" The brewer-woman said that she didn't know what chwerwlys was. Borrow explained that it was what the Saxons called wormwood, which word the woman must have recognised for she said; "Oh, wermod. There is not much wermod in my beer." Her explanation of why wormwood was put into beer suggests that it was used a hop substitute when hops were dear and that some folks preferred the taste to that of hops. This is all very peculiar because wormwood, *artemisia absinthium,* a bitter plant was originally used as a vermifuge, that's to say to kill worms, presumably intestinal worms. My Chambers dictionary also states that absinthe is flavoured with it and that the Old English name is wermod (in French 'vermouth'), the same word that the brewer-woman used.

Just before 2pm I came into the tiny hamlet of Ffair Rhos* where the map suggested there was a pub. I hurried the last mile in expectation of a pint, or two, to slake my considerable thirst, found the pub at the crossroads but quickly discovered that I'd not be drinking, for the pub had a 'Closed' notice in the window. To Borrow, Ffair Rhos was "a miserable village consisting of a few half-ruined cottages, situated on the top of a hill". To me it was an undistinguished place consisting of the pub, a chapel and some scruffy houses. The view, however, from the chapel, was magnificent. A vast stretch of country was visible even though the clouds were still hugging the hilltops. The steep and wooded scarp of Pen y Bannau, a fortified hilltop, hid the view of Strata Florida but I caught a distant glimpse of the Teifi meandering away to the west.

The footpath shortcut I'd intended to take just beyond the hamlet was clearly marked by a fingerpost but led into long wet grass. As I'd just stopped to change my wet socks, I opted to stay on the road where harebells and ragwort and blackberries and ferns decorated the verges down the hill towards the Teifi.

Pontrhydfendigaid* began as an unattractive rash of modern bungalows, soon followed by the Carmel Baptist Chapel (1872); council houses; a three storey, derelict warehouse; a long terrace of houses in drab greys and creams; a unisex hair salon; a church dated 1859; the Black Lion Hotel; another chapel and then the Red Lion Hotel. Well, this was a village of variety and contrast. Borrow found "much mire in the street; immense swine lay in the mire; women in Welsh hats stood in the mire". I saw no mire at all; in fact, the place looked very spick and span. I crossed the Teifi on a pretty, old stone-built, hump-backed bridge* beyond which I turned left to Strata Florida.

The lane that led from the village centre to Strata Florida Abbey wound unremarkably through riverside pasture land for two kilometres. Abruptly I came to the Abbey* at a bend in the road. Entry was via the usual 'sucker-trap' office and shop, though in this case it included a small area displaying artefacts found on the site.

The Abbey, now in the care of CADW (the Welsh agency for the care of historic sites), was initially founded in 1164 on a site nearby; the present Abbey buildings were erected around 1200. This remote Cistercian house was strongly supported by the native Welsh princes and became a focus for literary activity and influence. In 1165 Rhys ap Griffith, the Welsh ruler, commenced his support for Strata Florida and later other native Welsh rulers, too, made grants of land for abbey foundations and Cistercian expansion in Wales began to blossom. Unlike other monastic orders the Cistercians found much favour in Wales. One of their distinguishing features was their dependance on land to provide income. This included arable land for crops and pasture land for sheep rearing and for wool production, especially important in Wales. The Cistercians had no direct Norman links and their austerity and self-sufficiency made them natural successors to the early Welsh church system which had been destroyed by the Normans. Dafydd ap Gwylim, one of the finest poets to write in Welsh, is buried within the Abbey precinct.

The ruins are immaculately kept; the ruined walls, mostly only knee-high are weed-free and well mortared forming the rectangles of the original rooms whose floors are now lush and close-mown turf. Thus the ground plan of the Abbey is clearly visible. I was astonished by its geometric rectangularity, which was accentuated by its setting, surrounded as it was by peaceful open countryside of hills, trees and pasture which imposed no geometry on it whatsoever. The tranquillity of this remote setting made it easy to understand why the monks chose such a site. Although a fine relic, there was not much of architectural interest to see, apart from the main entrance arch* which still stood in most of its original ornate finery. It was, however, by no means comparable with Tintern, which was the first and richest of the Cistercian abbeys in Wales for there the walls and their magnificent windows are still standing roof-high.

Borrow was anxious to see Strata Florida Abbey, mainly, I get the impression, because it was the "last resting place of Dafydd ap Gwilym." He describes the scenery around the monastery in a dozen lines but of the ruins he merely writes: "Those scanty broken ruins compose all which remains of that celebrated monastery, in which kings, saints and mitred abbots were buried, and in which, or in whose precincts, was buried Dafydd ap Gwilym, the greatest genius of the Celtic race and one of the first poets of the world." He was evidently not very impressed with the Abbey ruins but I was. More of the ruins had doubtless been excavated since his visit. He then spent some time poking about the adjoining churchyard wondering where ap Gwilym's grave might be.

Having returned, like Borrow, to Pontrhydfendigaid I continued on the road to Tregaron. A row of fine Georgian stone houses lined the street up the hill whose period charm was rather spoilt by the row of ugly 1960s semis on the other side of the road. A drab garage, whose defunct solitary petrol pump leaned drunkenly into the street, featured a lone banger for sale for £450. The interior of the post office was invisible through the filthy, fly-blown glass of its window which was further obscured by blobs of dirty Blutack and curling yellow Sellotape. I passed yet another church by the war memorial.

Beyond the village was the Bryn y Gors Holiday Park, a euphemism for a caravan site, which was tucked away in the boggy marshland behind an ineffective screen of trees and bushes. The road was level and on the edge of the very flat river Teifi flood plain which widened out to the south into the extensive flatlands of the Cors Caron bog.There were still green and lumpy hills to my left on the eastern side of the Teifi valley, or at least there were until they disappeared into murk as the rain came down. Thank goodness for the umbrella.

By three-thirty I'd crossed onto the next map and the whole expanse of the Cors Caron came into view. Perfectly level, brown and lumpy with tussock and reeds dotted with small trees and bushes it was a veritable plain, evocative of the savannah grasslands of East Africa. It had a unique atmosphere, the Cors Caron bog. The stunted trees in the foreground obscured the plain behind. There was then a wide space where nothing could be seen, as if the middle distance had been erased, before the apparently very distant hills on the far side which were actually less than three kilometres away. The road marked the sharp edge of the bog at the abrupt foot of the eastern hills. As I walked I mused that I'd heard no Welsh spoken since leaving Machynlleth whereas Borrow had several encounters with folk who were bi-lingual or spoke no English. Aware that consonants mutate in Welsh depending on their associated case, I considered the connection between the name Tre-garon and Cors Caron and decided that Tregaron was the 'town on the Caron', the C having mutated to a G, or vice versa.

At the Cors Caron car park where the Nature Trail begins I found an information board. " *This is a National Nature Reserve. It is one of the finest examples of rare raised bogs in Europe. Peat has accumulated over the last ten thousand years to form a raised dome ten metres thick in places. The peat is formed from the remains of bog plants, especially mosses, which accumulate year by year in the waterlogged conditions. We welcome everyone, including wheelchair users, on the old railway walk. The walk to the bird hide normally takes about thirty minutes but you need a permit from the warden to enter other parts of the reserve. We want to encourage the water-loving plants to grow and to form peat. Local people used to cut peat here to burn as fuel for many years. We are now enclosing these areas with low embankments to prevent the water seeping away. Trees now grow in the dryer part of the bog and we will also be removing these."*

At four o'clock I reached the track to Maesllyn* where I could see a large, grey-rendered, two storey farmhouse about 300m from the old railway.There were some barns at the back, an orange tractor and the ubiquitous four-by-four parked in front. The farm sat in flat, rich grazing land, as it lay at the edge of the Cors Caron bog, thus it would be mostly peat. Just to the left of the farm track was a smallish lake which was doubtless the lake that Borrow refers to in his narrative.

Borrow had come what he reckoned was about four miles from Pontrhydfendigaid and it was now dark. He saw by the glimmer of moonlight "what appeared to be a large sheet of water" and went on for a minute or two when he saw "two or three houses on the left which stood nearly opposite to the object which I had deemed to be water". An odd turn of phrase this, for surely a lake is unmistakable even by moonlight. Unless Borrow mistook his left for his right, the farmhouse I had seen west of the lake was not the house where he then stopped to enquire the name of the place for he says that it was on his left, that is to the east of the road. Anyway, he knocked on the door of the main house and conversed with the woman who opened it about the lake, its fish and its "water-cow". I saw no building to the east of the road hereabouts, so who knows whether he was confused, whether I was unobservant or whether the house had been demolished?

He then "rushed on at great speed" and met another traveller with whom he conversed all the way to Tregaron. He learned from this "stout, burly man" that Tregaron was famous for its ham and for the notorious robber Twm Shon Catti, that Robin Hood of Cardiganshire. Borrow's narrative devotes some five pages to this hero of Welsh folk history, as related by Borrow's walking companion on the dark road to Tregaron.

From the lake I could see the full width of the flat, brown plain of the bog, studded with bushes and stunted trees, which began behind the farm where the grazing land sloped down to meet it where a line of scrub formed a vague boundary between the two. I could not see the River Teifi which was not far away, ambling its way through the sepia flatness.

I continued along the former railway which was now a gravelled path, flat, and providing easy walking which was a delight after so much road work. Soft underfoot and safe. Mallard quacked on the lake; the air was full of the bleating of sheep; hazel and hawthorn bordered the lake whose far side was streaked with irises and bull-rushes; on the water floated the flat saucers of water lilies; mare's tail stood tall at the water margin. A marsh at the lake's end was resplendent with magnificent golden irises and the huge yellow orbs of marsh marigolds. I walked into a warm and scented corridor between borders of the dense creamy froth of meadow sweet; ahh, what a treat for the senses! For 200 metres that exquisite, subtle, nostril-expanding scent of the flowers wafted on the breeze whilst I strolled along in a narcotic daze. Tall, sturdy umbells with tops big enough to use as rain shelters grew where the meadow-sweet finally petered out.

I passed a boardwalk leading into the bog, zigzagging its way between the bushes: the official pedestrian entry into the Reserve whose entrance was under a triple arch constructed from carved tree limbs. Clover and hawksbit and foxgloves and vetch, buttercups and daisies, yarrow, rose-bay and seeding grasses swayed in a mist of colour along the borders of the track. In a while I passed another lake, not shown on the map, where dragonflies and damsel flies whirred and hovered among the rushes and marestails. Finally the track evidently entered onto private land for it was blocked by a substantial mess of barbed wire and so I had to climb a fence, ascend the steep field to the road and force my way through the hawthorn hedge onto the highway. It was suddenly most unpleasant to be back on the road; the ever-present danger of traffic; the lack of anything interesting to see; the hard surface underfoot. Now and then, through gaps in the roadside hedge, I could catch a glimpse of the country to the right and soon saw that the bog had ended and the river had swung away from the road off to the west. Undistinguished farmland lay to my right and gentle hills to my left.

At four-thirty, eight hours after leaving Ponterwyd, I entered the bungalowed outskirts of Tregaron. This was the usual unprepossessing, modern and characterless entry into villages and towns in this part of Wales. Sheep dog trials were in progress just before the first houses, which I paused for a while to watch, expecting to marvel anew at the consummate skill of one man and his dog in shepherding a group of wayward and recalcitrant ewes into a pen. However on this occasion I was astonished to witness the sheep outwitting and apparently outrunning the sheepdog with farcical and chaotic results. The shepherd, meanwhile, was stamping his feet, waving his crook and blowing his whistle in vain. Hey, one up to the sheep!

The suburb of neat, orderly little bungalows in tidy rows was made noisy by the hum and roar of lawnmowers. It could have been anywhere; it was not Tregaron particularly; it was not Wales particularly; the twee bungalows could have been in Surbiton or Macclesfield. I arrived, at a quarter to five, in the almost-pretty square in Tregaron where the Talbot Arms overlooked the bustle at the end of market day. I checked that I had a room before ordering two pints and taking them outside to quench a very considerable thirst. I sat in front of the hotel and enjoyed the attractive, brightly painted buildings, mostly Georgian, that formed the square. The stall holders were packing up their unsold goods; kids were performing wheelies on bikes; there was a constant coming and going at the Spar shop across the way and it was good to sit down in the knowledge that I had to walk no more that day having covered nearly nineteen miles.

The cafe at Pontrhydygroes

Cors Caron Bog and the infant River Teifi

The Hafod Arms Hotel at Devil's Bridge

The Talbot Inn at Tregaron

A BETTER ROUTE IN OUR TIMES

There is no doubt about the route that Borrow took onward from Tregaron for he lists the settlements he passed through: Abercoed, Abercarven, Nantderven and Llanddewi Brefi. These villages are all identifiable on the modern map so it is obvious that he walked the line what is now the B4343. He discourses lengthily about this Llandewi Brefi because "in the fifth century one of the most remarkable ecclesiastical convocations which the world has ever seen was held in this secluded spot." Briefly, a celebrated teacher of theology from Pembrokeshire, called Dewi, was summoned to arbitrate on a matter of religious dogma. Dewi's treatise was accepted by the "convocation". (I was earlier musing on collective nouns: a 'convocation of eagles'). As a result Dewi later became the primate of Wales and gave his name to St David's. Five hundred years later several churches were dedicated to him, one of which was the church called Llan Dewi Brefi which was built above the cell in which Dewi composed his seminal treatise.

Borrow then continued to Lampeter, along the same line to the east of the Teifi, where he says that the country "presented nothing remarkable" and that he " met on the road nothing worthy of being recorded". Boring country indeed for him to have dismissed some seven miles in such a way. Having visited the church college at Lampeter he then continued towards Llandovery following the approximate line of what is now the A482. He may have taken what is now a minor road at Cwmann, (which is nowadays a depressing linear roadside development) where the main road makes a swing to the south to avoid a steep hill and enters the valley of the Nant Eiddig. He stopped at a small village which he was told was called "Pen-something" (another vague place-name from the philologist) which could have been Penybryn.

The scenery as far as the pass at grid reference SN614437 did not impress Borrow for he wrote:

" I was soon amongst desolate hills of a wretched russet colour exhibiting no other signs of life and cultivation than here and there a miserable field and vile-looking hovel. There were no songs of birds, no voices of rills." He was evidently following the line of the A482 for he came to a village whose name he learnt was Dolwen which is now called Darlwyn and is indeed "about halfway down the hill". Further on he spoke to a pedestrian, an Irishwoman called Mary Bane, and then to a Welshman who was employed at Dolcothi, a place whose name Borrow knew for it was the birthplace of his friend, the poet Lewis Glyn Cothi. Presently, Borrow and his Welsh companion came to the `Pont y Twrch' which is now a modern road bridge over the Afon Twrch close to where the Roman road Sarn Helen meets the A482. Borrow stopped for the night at the "Inn of the Pump Saint" which was, without doubt, situated at the present day hamlet of Pumsaint on the A482. ('Pump' is the Welsh word for five).

As for me, I had already done more than enough road walking in the steps of the estimable George and so resolved to find a more interesting, more stimulating and less dangerous and stressful route across country. I decided to follow his route as far as Llandewi Brefi and then go via lanes and footpaths in the most direct line possible to Caio where I had booked at a B and B. This would take me over the hills and down into the upper Twrch valley, then up again and down into the valley of the Cothi which I would descend to Dolaucothi. A short rounding of a spur would then take me to Caio. It was to turn out to be a strenuous day.

I left the Talbot Inn just after nine and passed the statute of Henry Richard, the great Welsh philanthropist, who was born in Tregaron. The inscription read: *I've always been mindful of three things: not to forget the language of my country and the people and cause of my country, and to neglect no opportunity of defending the character and promoting the interest of my country. My hope for abatement of the war system lies in the permanent conviction of the people rather than the policies of cabinets or the discussions of parliaments."* A serious creed, indeed, to ponder as I walked out of the town into the mist and drizzle on the road to Llandewi Brefi. Henry Richard evidently should have been listed along with ham and Twm Shone Catti as items for which Tregaron is famous.

I had considered reaching Llandewi Brefi by means of a lane, tracks and paths up the hillside but the visibility was so poor and the vegetation so wet that I could see little point or pleasure in leaving the B4343. I mused that, apart from the barmaid in the Talbot, I'd heard no Welsh spoken in Tregaron but only English with a strong Welsh accent. The town square had been noisy with rumbustious youth the previous evening for, as usual, youngsters seemed to have nothing better to do, or anywhere else to do it. An alarm in a car parked in the square had started to screech at twenty to midnight, continued for twenty minutes, stopped for five and then began again. This was a serious interruption to what I most needed: a good night's sleep.

I passed the hospital, most of which was a two-storey, ranch-style building in grey brick set adjacent to a much older, three-storey, grey stuccoed edifice. The road was sufficiently quiet for me soon to be able to hear the River Teifi gently singing over its pebble bed and for me to take my eyes off the road long enough to enjoy the occasional glimpses of its meanders through the trees. Borrow states that he walked the stretch from Tregaron in forty-five minutes so I was intrigued to see how long it would take me.

Abercoed* was a well-kept former farmhouse with some carefully restored brick and stone outbuildings. Neat and tidy they were, except where the walls faced away from the house where the stonework didn't seem to have had any attention for decades. The mist had descended even lower to restrict visibility to less than three hundred metres and to create a still, damp mugginess that made me sweat profusely. Buzzards mewed in that plaintive way they have, invisible in the murk overhead.

Abercarven* featured an odd eroded stack of shalestone in front of the farmhouse, a very bizarre feature for it stood about three metres high and I could see no reason for it. The road wound pleasantly along the hillside, following its contours at the edge of the river plain.

Nant y Derwen* was still a working farm for slurry was leaking from the end of one of the old stone barns that had arched doorways and high-level windows. The smart whitewashed farmhouse sat rather incongruously looking over a scruffy and untidy farmyard. At Pant a small, man-made lake lay still and grey, tucked into the landscape. The farmyard was full of bleating sheep milling about in apparent total confusion whilst three men tried to do something to them but what, exactly, I couldn't say. A sign said "Pant Farm Trout Lake" so this was a bit of enterprising agricultural diversity.

At ten o'clock exactly I entered the customary rash of modern bungalows that formed the outskirts of Llandewi Brefi*, passed council housing, village green and bus-stop shelter but no people apparently inhabited the place for it was deserted. I passed a gigantic statue of a soldier acting as a war memorial and a graveyard devoid of church and arrived in the centre five minutes later. It had taken me fifty-one minutes from Tregaron: six minutes longer than Borrow which I found rather galling but then he was ten years younger than I at the time of the walk.

The village centre was an attractive milieu with well-kept stone terraced houses and a Bethesda chapel built in 1826. One pedestrian, an old man tottering along with a stick on his morning constitutional, was the only sign of human life I saw. The main church was large, stone-built with a massive tower capped by a short pointed spire and seemed far too large for such a small community. The presence of yet another chapel confirmed that this had indeed been a hotbed of religious fervour. The community centre, however, was a crass example of gruesome modern utilitarian community architecture without any visual merit whatsoever and which must have been approved by a committee grossly insensitive to the vernacular.

Leaving the village I met only the third pedestrian I had encountered all day, a young lad running down the hill. I took a lane which led very steeply up and round the hillside immediately to the south the village. As I ascended, the visibility lessened until I was walking in a cocoon of mist dense enough to touch. In a while I turned left to continue steeply up into the hills. There were one or two scattered houses along the laneside, including a remote bed and breakfast, but soon there was nothing but the quiet, looming mist and a short vista of boggy ground and fir trees. Very dreary. By ten fifty-seven I'd reached the corner of the wood at Esgair Goch where the map informed me that some vastly extensive plantations began.

Whilst toiling uphill in the mist I was amazed and shocked to suddenly see what appeared to be a large brown bear lumbering down the lane, out of the mist, directly at me. And immediately after this monster hove into view the air was split by a woman's shout. I froze to the spot, imagining all kinds of horror scenarios, but soon realised that this was a large, very large, Andean-type dog, in fact the biggest dog I'd ever seen, which soon slowed and approached me with caution. I stood stock still, the dog's owner appeared and said, as dog owners nearly always do: "It's all right, he won't hurt you". To which I replied, as I always do: "Yes, you know that madam, but I don't". She had been calling the beast to order, of which it took not the slightest notice but believed that I was a plaything, so my legs were now covered in dog-paw-mud and there was slobber on my chest.I made off as fast as possible, not being able to think where these two had come from, but soon passed a small car at the side of the road. Hardly room in that thing for a dog that size, I thought, but I could understand why she had got well out of the village before letting it out! I mean, for God's sake, what on earth is the appeal of a dog as big as a donkey. Why would one want a dog that size?

I ambled on shrouded in mist and pine trees through a landscape that I couldn't see, feeling that this was truly wild Wales. With some relief I reached spot height 452 metres which was the highest point I would visit that day. Here, oppressive conifers crowded in closely on both sides of the road but I couldn't see their tops: it was a darkly grim place made all the grimmer by the sight of a dumped TV set in the ditch. My mood was lightened by the sight of a sparkling, dew-jewelled network of spider's webs clinging to the heather along both verges. The plants looked for all the world as if they had been frosted. There must have been thousands of spiders busy overnight. How did they manage to spin such an intricate, perfect web pattern with such delicate material? John Clare wrote some lines about this:

"The morning comes, the drops of dew
   hand on the grass and bushes too;
the sheep more eager bite the grass
   whose moisture gleams like drops of glass;
the heifer licks-in grass and dew
   that make her drink and fodder too."

As I descended into the valley of the Twrch, the forest became more varied with ash, oak, cherry and birch breaking the coniferous monotony. Towards the bottom of the wood the road crossed a stream, which oddly seemed to be running around the hillside not down it, and passed into an eerie woodland landscape where loggers had clear-felled an area but, for some reason, left the occasional dead defoliated tree standing, eerily wreathed in mist. This evoked images of the devastation of trench warfare and saturation shelling. There was the mud, the splintered trunks, the spare needle-less trees, the dismal and depressing surroundings.

The tiny hamlet of Llechau Uchaf consisted of three dwellings, all uninhabited, but one was evidently in the throes of renovation. Someone thought enough of the place to give it its own name board; it is not named on the map. By noon I'd reached the valley floor where the road finally levelled off and where I had lost enough height to drop below the mist level. The view, however, was not exciting: a typical upland valley with rough pasture and plantations, drab in the grey light and not inspiring of poetic description. As I turned up the track to Sychnant I was startled by a field mouse that sprinted across the way almost under my feet and in so doing disturbed a peacock's feather. An odd object to find just here, I thought. But the explanation was only just around the next bend for there, all alone, was a fine peacock in full plumage, pecking by the trackside. Why he was there was a mystery, as the farm at Sychnant was certainly no stately home. There I took the footpath across the field where sheep had, I was pleased to see, grazed the turf short so I'd not be wading through tall, wet grass.

The FC plantation on the hilltop above Sychnant had been shoddily clear felled leaving the usual dead trees standing in isolation amidst the chaos of stumps and cut branches: the customary bombsite forest. A track led into this mess where I was surprised to find that I was again above 300m. The landscape in this former woodland was a peculiar mixture of hayfields, sheep grazing, patches of unimproved ground with birch and alder scrub, gorse thickets and marsh grass and reeds and a disused quarry all of which now appeared as if it had never been forested. But my map told me differently and I soon found that all of the forest shown had been clear-felled. The track became tarmac at the edge of the former wood. It was unearthly quiet as I descended into the valley of the Afon Fanafas, no bird song, no sound of human activity; it seemed very remote and isolated.

I sat on a bridge abutment near Tynant to air my feet and take in liquid. Washing was on the line at Tynant; a quadbike suddenly roared into view down the hillside. The dale was pleasantly green, gently hilly, softly wooded and very peaceful. I passed several valley farms spaced about half a kilometre apart but the country was devoid of human life but full of the sound of running water. What a balm for the soul was this placid and sombre country.

By noon I was on the track through Garth farm where, unusually,   large flocks of chickens, ducks and geese were pecking and squabbling around the buildings. There were sheep in profusion: sheep with floppy ears, black sheep, brown sheep, variegated sheep, small sheep, big sheep; so many different sheep that I thought this must be a rare-breeds farm. I was entertained to watch, in a pen at the back of the farm, two men waving their arms. like string-operated puppets. at a bunch of sheep in a vain attempt to get the animals to do something that they were reluctant to do. No specialised skills for manipulating sheep then. This was another pretty and peaceful valley but visually ruined by the hideous metal-clad barns on the hillside at Bwlchgwynant. These seemed needlessly high and elaborate with arched and pointed tops. Yet another was under construction. Were there any planning restrictions here on agricultural building, I wondered, or was it the same as in Hereford where it seemed that farmers could ruin the appearance of the countryside in any ugly way they chose.

I had chosen to follow this track to the edge of the FC plantation above the Afon Fanagoed and then follow what was shown on the map as a path through the wood. However this turned out to be a tactical error for when I arrived at the wood edge, the line of the path was only dimly visible: it was evidently an overgrown forest ride or extraction lane which was now virtually impassable due to the brambles, scrub and nettles. I could see no alternative to bash on through it, and what an awful struggle it was. I was tripped by brambles, scratched and torn by them, stung by nettles, plagued by flies, spattered with mud and rendered almost incapable by exhaustion and sweat. As I toiled I sensed, for the first time, that there is something truly forbidding about these huge, dark, silent conifer woods where the sun never shines and nothing moves or sings. *("In the pines, in the pines where the sun never shines she shivered the whole night through". (From 'Where did You Sleep Last Night' by Lead Belly))*. An air of menace seemed to drift between the densely packed black trunks, an air made worse from time to time by a foul and foetid stench, as if something had died and was decomposing. Ugh, what an experience this was turning into.

After five hundred metres of fight, now high-stepping over brambles, now ducking through the trees I came to the end of it to find myself on the edge of a large clearing, on a dirt track but unable to orientate myself or decide in which direction to go. More by luck than navigational skill I finally found my way onto a foully muddy track which led to a group of buildings where vehicles were parked. A group of youngsters were sitting round a table outside and evidently having a good laugh. At me, I wondered? The track led on through narrow pasture, heavily flanked on both sides by the forest - I wasn't out of the trees yet.

At the crossing of the Fanagoed stream there was no vehicle bridge, merely a ford, but for pedestrians there was a footbridge leading onto the tarmac surface beyond. Six parallel lines of damp on the road at the road junction at Abermangoed gave me pause for conjecture as to their origin. The tarmac looked...well, sort of clean, kind of swept. Surely a road sweeper hadn't been up here in this remote country lane, sweeping the road? That was certainly what the marks suggested but what an appalling waste of council-tax payers' money. What idiot had ordered this? Why on earth would you send a road-sweeper up here? And to do a shoddy job too, for I'd stepped on two muddy twigs that the machine had missed! A little later all this was confirmed for I caught up the road sweeping lorry which I couldn't pass as it blocked the whole width of the lane. A good excuse to stop for a breather and a drink.

The sweeper having noisily disappeared, I walked on down the Cothi valley past a man strimming bracken at his field boundaries, doubtless in an attempt to keep the wretched weed at bay. I'd never seen this particular agricultural activity before. At three-thirty I reached the affluent-looking stone houses at Landre where red woodwork vied with geraniums in beds and pots to be the brightest objects in a grey and sunless day. A farm house and a group of immaculate barns facing a well-scrubbed farmyard formed the cleanest, best-kept farm that I'd seen all week. A muck spreader in a barn led me to think that this prosperous farm had cattle as well as sheep.

As I approached Brunant I heard some extraordinary sounds, presumably animal, that were new to me. I wondered at length what these unearthly screechings might be but I was soon enlightened by the sight of three ostriches in a wired pen adjacent to the farm buildings. An ususual sight in Wales, ostriches. There were other exotic birds in pens making peculiar mewings that I couldn't identify. Outside the entrance to Brunant Mansion a Plaid Cymru poster was affixed to a telephone pole. Dolaucothi Farm to which Borrow refers, looked much like any other farm hereabouts with whacking great grey-metal barns and some older built of corrugated asbestos. A little further, some ornamental trees, cedars, deodars, redwoods, huge sycamores, ash and copper beech led me to believe that there was an estate here, perhaps Dolaucothi Estate. I could dimly glimpse, through the dense vegetation of bushes, rhododendrons and trees, some tents or caravans or other camping-type installations.

At three-forty I turned off the road to take a footpath through National Trust land which led pleasantly through sun-dappled ash and oak woodland but the path had been rendered virtually impassable because horses had churned the path into an appalling muddy slurry where I sank to my ankles in the muck. I shortly came to a cave in a cliff on my left the mouth of which was barred by a locked gate over the entrance to the tunnel beyond. The bedding planes of the shaly rock were vertical; stunted oaks grew in the rock above the dark and gaping cave mouth. Close by was a short length of tramway track bearing a couple of rusting wagons aligned with an arch through which, presumably, the wagons ran at one time carrying the output from the cave. A mine, perhaps? A glance at the map showed "Roman Gold Mines" and so I assumed that gold had been mined here, in this pretty dingle, but later than Roman times for I'm sure they didn't construct tramways. It was all a mystery.

In the cwm below there appeared to be some sort of tourist attraction. Further inspection revealed a flat area containing a car park, a high metal gantry frame supporting a pair of winding wheels, a network of tram tracks below, a building with a yellow roof and two red corugated iron barns. People were ambling about but I was reluctant to descend for I was by now extremely tired and didn't fancy the toil back up the hill. Some kids were sounding a horn or klaxon, a relic of the mining era, I assumed, in an area where lengths of track sections were stacked. The Dolaucothi Gold Mine Visitor Centre, I surmised.

In a while the path rejoined the road which I followed eastwards towards a blue sky that was reluctantly appearing from the murk and mist I'd endured all day. The hills had lost that dead, sullen, secretive look that they have when the mist is down and had become lighted, alive with colour. I walked passed a sign which said ' National Trust Gwarnoethle' and into that distressing varying whine of chainsaws and a crunching, ripping noise which, together, filled the afternoon with the hideous racket of tree destruction. Was this the NT at work?

The descent into Caio gave a remarkable view of the village church and its massive tower with a battlemented top. The village tumbled, higgledy-piggledy, down the hillside and in due course I was welcomed to Caio by the village sign in English and in Welsh. A pretty line of terraced cottages adorned with hanging flower baskets terminated in the pub opposite the church. The pub was closed, there was no-one about to ask and so, in search of my booked accommodation, I walked up past the church and some houses to where I spied a bed and breakfast sign. Fortunately a woman was in her garden, told me that she was not what I was looking for and gave me directions to a house some distance from the village. Oh, dear, I thought I'd done walking for the day! Returning past the pub I asked a man sat in his car outside the hostelry if it was open, to which he shook his head. I wearily walked back through the village and then past the entrance to Glanyrannell farm where an aged milk churn inscribed CWS stood atop a stone-built platform. At the stream bridge just beyond this feature I paused for a drink and a rest for I was exhausted and demoralised by the extra distance I still had to go. The bridge was built by Llandovery District Council in 1925 and was now well-weathered.

Trying to remember the instructions I had been given, I called at a bungalow about half a kilometre further on where I waited, in the utter silence of the late afternoon, for some four minutes for the door to be opened. I was told that this was not the my destination, so I apologised, and walked on. A little further along the lane, at twenty to five, I came to a bed and breakfast sign and the name ' Arwel Deg' so I knew that I'd finally arrived. It was by now a hot afternoon as a result of which I was very tired and sweaty. On my way to the front door I vaguely noticed a parked car, but paid it no attention as all I wanted to do was get in, get my boots off and lie down. However, there was no answer from repeated rings at the door bell and so I turned away from the house to sit down and ponder my next move. It was then that I noticed that the occupant of the parked car was the same guy that I'd spoken to outside the village pub.

This man, Simon Long-Price, was also booked in for bed and breakfast and had also tried the door and got no reply. We thought it peculiar that there was apparently no-one at home, so I went and peered in the windows. No bodies on the floor, no bodies alive or dead anywhere. We decided to wait until five fifteen and then seek accommodation elsewhere. To pass the time, we talked. I told him what I was doing and he told me that he was staying for a few nights whilst researching his family history, that of the Long-Prices of Talley. I was in august company it seemed for not only was he landed gentry but also related to Sir Robert Peel, he of the Metropolitan Police Force.

At five-twenty we gave up, I got into his car, all sweaty and odiferous, and he drove to the pub at Felin Newydd on the A482. This pub was closed too, but by dint of shouting at an open window I managed to achieve the success of a head appearing at a bedroom window. Enquiring about Arwel Deg I was told that Mrs George would not be home until gone six. I also learned that the Dolaucothi Arms, the inn at Pumsaint where Borrow stayed the night, no longer provided accommodation. So I got back in the car and we went to the pub at Caio, the Brunant Arms, which was still closed. After more shouting, and knocking on the door, a young woman appeared who informed us that the pub didn't open until six. I begged some tea, the afternoon being now very warm and I had a very considerable thirst after the day's walk. So we took tea in the garden at the back and very pleasant it was too, though it did little to slake my thirst. At six we had a pint, or two, and then returned to Arwel Deg where Mrs George was now at home. After a shower and a change of clothes, Mrs George was kind enough to drive us to the pub for supper. Simon didn't, rightly, want to drive as he wanted to drink.

We had an excellent meal, courtesy of David and Samantha Phillips who had only been publicans for six days, after which Simon began his research by interviewing the older drinkers about their knowledge of the Talley estate. Whilst drinking my two post-prandial pints, which I felt that I'd earned, I watched Simon talking to the elders of the village whilst copiously drinking. In due course he used his mobile phone to call Mrs George who duly arrived to ship us to our beds. Gosh, what an entertaining and diverting evening it had been, but all a bit too demanding after a day's walk of some thirty kilometres.

Tenth day

RITES OF WAY

I had passed the night at Caio and Borrow at Pumsaint, but these two villages are less than two kilometres apart so, although I was now following my own preferred route in this age of dangerous roads, I wasn't too far from his footsteps.

Of Pumsaint Borrow wrote: "The village consists of little more than half a dozen houses. The inn is a good specimen of an ancient Welsh hostelry. Its gable is to the road and its front to a little space on one side of the way. At a little distance up the road is a blacksmith's shop. The country around is interesting: on the north-west is a fine wooded hill - to the south a valley through which flows the Cothi, a fair river, the one whose murmur had come so pleasingly upon my ear in the depth of night."

The hill to which he refers was probably Pen Lan-dolau, which is still wooded today. His description of the inn roughly corresponds to the format of the present pub. After leaving the village Borrow visited a "gentleman's seat", belonging so he was told to a Mr Johnes (the same name as the man at Hafod, curiously enough, but possibly the same person). Borrow "advanced along the avenue of very noble oaks". He noted " a beautiful brook running north and south; fine wooded hills to the east; the house, a plain but comfortable gentleman's seat with wings." (His description of the house, typical of his era, could also be that of a chair, or seat). There is really no clue in his text as to the exact location of this estate, for his timings are characteristically vague: "presently I came to.........a little distance.........after some miles...........in a little time" and so forth.

After leaving the gentleman's seat he crossed Pont y Rhanedd, the bridge over the river of that name and passed by a "lofty mountain which appeared to have three heads". Although I can't identify either of these with certainty on the modern map, it is likely, knowing the possibilities for misunderstanding in the pronunciation of Welsh names, that the river was the Afon Annell and that the 'mountain' was the hill immediately to the east of my night's lodging which has three ring contours, or isolation contours, near its summit implying three separate tops. It is, however, evident that he followed the line of the modern A482 for he writes: "After some miles I came to where the road divided into two.......one by Porthyrhyd and one by Llanwrda". This is without doubt the road junction at the present day Maestwynog. "The distance by the first was six miles and a half, by the latter eight and a half. Feeling quite the reverse of tired I chose the longest road, namely the one by Llanwrda". So he chose to follow the valley of the Afon Dulais which he describes as "a romantic winding dell overhung with trees of various kinds". If one can ignore the nastiness of the main road now in this "dell", his description is still apt. He was told by "a tall man" whom he met that the valley was known as Cwm Dwr Llanwrda, or the Watery Vale of Llanwrda, and also that the snow was two feet deep at Sebastopol.

In due course he passed through Llanwrda, "a pretty village with a singular-looking church, close to which stood an enormous yew" and turned north in the valley of the Towy. He "journeyed past beautiful hills, partly cultivated, partly covered with wood, and here and there dotted with farmhouses and gentlemen's seats; green pastures which descended nearly to the river". After about four miles he came to "a noble suspension bridge" and shortly entered Llandovery where he "put up" at the Castle Inn.

As for me, I'd decided to avoid the horrors of the A482 and follow a quieter route to Llandovery. I'd perused the map and worked out a fairly direct line using lanes and footpaths but firstly, to avoid the dreaded main road, I had to take a path uphill which led directly to Maescadog thus avoiding three km of road walking. This would be the first of two long and steep ascents. It was obvious from the map exactly where this path left the lane that I was following back toward Caio but on the ground I could find no trace of it whatsoever. There was no finger-post, no stile and no break in the dense and impenetrable, stockproof hazel and hawthorn hedge along the roadside. I walked past the spot three times to be certain but reluctantly gave up and continued along the lane. Huh, so much for access to the countryside and the efficiency of the local authority's footpath department. But I did find a path to the village, furnished with kissing-gates and leading across water meadows, starting by an elegant mansion in classical style with a porticoed front door and set in extensive grounds thick with rhododendrons. The path field had recently been cut for hay so the wet grass was short enough not to soak through my boots.

The Caio sewage treatment works boasted a large solar panel on a pole by the side of the stream - surely that couldn't generate enough electricity to power the filter beds, could it? Before joining the road at the east side of the village I passed an ancient Morris Minor and an Austin A40, both dating from the early sixties, slumped amongst the weeds by the river bridge. A vintage car enthusiast or merely a junk yard?

The ascent to the east from Caio was appallingly steep; in fact the road gained 100 metres of height in under a kilometre of distance, a gradient of 1 in 10, so I was gasping and sweating almost immediately. As I struggled up the hill I thought that, due to the dense network of roads and lanes throughout England and Wales, in the lowlands at least, and due to the ubiquity of the motor vehicle, nowhere could now be truly described as 'wild', or not in the sense that Borrow meant. However, by comparison with southern and central England the roads were not busy and the countryside had changed little since the 1850s so there were still similarities with the terrain that he experienced. At the hilltop I tottered into a pale and watery sunshine and paused to enjoy the view back to the village which was a hundred metres below. It was a complex landscape of valley and hill, of folded woodland and sloping pasture, of solid hedgerow and compact copse, of blanket plantations and bare summits. The vast plantation to the north was evidently a working forest because a gargantuan lorry stacked to the heavens with shaven logs pulled out from the forest entrance ahead of me, occupying the full width of the lane. The driveway entrance to Cilgawod farm was not the usual battered, sagging gate leading to a bleak cross-field track but, to my amazement it was a blaze of colour. Someone, presumably Mrs Farmer, had furnished the bell-mouth with pots and planters stuffed full of snapdragons, petunias, alyssum and love-in-the-mist , and others whose names escaped me. Bedding plants along the fence splay added to the riot of blues, reds and yellows. Well, an extraordinary effort especially on such a quiet lane where there were very few passers-by on foot and not many in vehicles.

I passed Maescadog at half past nine to the mewing of buzzards which were hidden overhead by the canopy of a stately avenue of mature beech trees. The scenery was soft, gentle hill country, mostly grazing land patched with coniferous woods and striped with lines of deciduous trees and wild hedgerows; scattered farms nestled in the green pleats; the ubiquitous sheep, in great profusion, safely grazed. I shortly entered the hamlet of Aberbowlan where four large and apparently aggressive Alsatians rushed frantically to and fro behind a fence doing their best to frighten me to death and creating a hideous din of barking and growling in the peaceful morning. I took a track which led straight up and over the hill in front, because the low level path which followed the contour of the base of the hill was completely invisible and I could see no way to get onto it. The pleasant grassy track climbed another hundred metres but after ten minutes of hard, sweaty work the angle eased.

I paused there where the land levelled off; the dogs at Aberbowlan were still giving voice; the bracken to either side was at its most rampant. This was dry upland grassland speckled with gorse, open common-land, and the view was wide and far. The complex geography showed itself in the fold upon fold of hill and dale, the woods and hedges mistily fading into the distance, the sweeping bald tops of Mynydd Mallaen, the two spreading

124

plantations of Caio Forest. Dog noise apart, it was a serenely peaceful spot, up there in a gentle breeze and morning sunshine.

William Barnes wrote, in 'The Hill Shade':
"At such a time, of year and day,
    in ages gone, that steep hill brow
cast down an evening shade, that lay
    in shape the same as lies there now:
though then no shadows wheeled around
    the things that now are on the ground."

To my surprise, in such a remote and beautiful location, I came upon an abandoned rusting field roller of enormous dimensions, at the side of the track and then more disused agricultural machinery in the shape of a dilapidated hay rake whose tines were decorated with dollops of manure and against which a battered tractor radiator was leaning, as if for comfort. The remains of a lorry with a wooden chassis showed that this stuff had been rotting here for fifty years or more; the body and tracks of a wrecked digger sat proudly on a little knoll; a distorted metal shape, tangled and mashed beyond recognition seemed to have suffered some appallingly violent assault. Stonechats whistled and clacked at me, fluttering along from bracken top to gorse sprig to fence post, imparting a little cheer into this sad museum of long-disused machines. I stepped into the bracken to inspect another mechanical conundrum, partly hidden amongst the fronds, which appeared to be an archaic threshing machine whose former ferric glory was now crumbling oxide. Well, it seemed that the local farmers had just brought their implements up here and dumped them when they were no longer needed.

This agricultural graveyard was a reminder that 150 years ago, Borrow would have walked through this landscape completely without the sound of mobile machines. Once he left industrial areas in the towns, where fixed steam and water powered machines would have created noise, he'd have heard no din made by internal combustion engines. Hardly imaginable, that, because now one is rarely free of the sound of machinery, whether road vehicles, farm vehicles or aircraft. Some of the latter were now making the skies hideous as our boys in blue went through their practise flights. And, sure enough, as I began the descent to Porthyrhyd, the roar of a tractor in the fields to the right competed with the jets to shatter the peace of the day. I was a little mollified to enjoy the view of a valley to the left, leading up into the bare hills, a wild and noble valley as Borrow would have said, meandering steeply up and away from me, delineated strongly by the line of dense bush and trees which fringed either side of its stream.

The descending track was, unusually, exposed shaly bedrock bearing no vegetation at all, with a resemblance to limestone pavement. Shallow soils. It led me into Porthyrhyd where a dozen or so newish houses did no favours to the older stone houses. The post office, dated 1906, was one no longer but still bore the title, and sat next to a handsome chapel. The presence of a farm at the road junction in the village suggested that this remote settlement had grown around the farm.

My route beyond took me into a plantation of thickly packed spruce called Garreg Fawr; a typically gloomy, oppressive and dank bit of coniferous woodland. The lane skirted round a small hill, following a sparkling stream whose banks were lush with wild flowers. The wood had become suddenly much more attractive for beech, hazel, willow, alder now grew amongst the dark northern aliens. Near Carregfechan I left the road for a farm track at the end of which the map showed a footpath leading across the fields towards Wern. Well, at the end of the track there were no finger-posts, no waymarkers, no sign at all of the correct line of the right of way, nor were there any stiles to mark the route. So I got out my compass, took a bearing off the map and followed it as best as I could. I halted where the land began to drop away down to the valley of the Afon Mynys where the view was of gentle pasture land cloaked with an abundance of native trees in pleasing natural groupings and I mused on the shortcomings of the local authority's obligation to mark and maintain public rights of way.

I had more difficulty a little further on and, uncharacteristically, lost my way completely in a jungle of head-high bracken surrounding a complex of deep-cut stream gullies. I finally reached the crossroads at Wern, hot and bothered, by means of a private access road. A few waymarkers across this complex terrain would have helped no end and kept me on the line where I had a legal right to be. A foot and mouth warning notice, covered in mould and dated May 2001, was stapled to a gatepost at the junction. They were slow around here alright. Why on earth hadn't someone taken it down?

I was dismayed to see another very steep ascent ahead; closer inspection of the map would have warned me of this as I was able to calculate a gradient of 1 in 5! Argh, it turned out to be the steepest of the day. I watched the sweat dripping off my face and onto my boots as I struggled to gain height. I dimly perceived another weed-battler strimming bracken in a paddock by the road. The footpath off to the right, which I could have taken, was not marked in any way. Just at the house on the hill there were, unbelievably, two strimmers and a lawn mower at work.

At eleven forty I paused at the entrance drive to Pen Rhiw at the top of the ascent to try to recover my composure after the steepest ascent of the whole walk. I was on the 210 metre contour, the altitude of which afforded me a spectacular view of the hill mass of Mynydd Mallaen, which at 450 metres, was a considerably high range for hereabouts. Its wild, rounded tops enclosed the deep-cut and rugged valley that led into it - the Afon Gwenlais.This massif, from this viewpoint, was as impressive as anything in my home terrain of the Welsh border country. Further west I could plainly see the forest in the Afon Fanagoed valley that I'd fought through the previous day. It was a very calm, very green, very unpopulated rural view much as I'd had on the other two preceding hilltops. In front, the road pointed directly at another bare, steep and intriguing hill, annotated merely as 'Fforest' on the map and 341 metres high. It looked like an interesting walk, up there, but now the way would lead down into the valley of the Towy and to Llandovery.

At grid reference SN738 358 the map showed a footpath leaving the road at a sharp bend. I wasted some ten minutes trying to find the exact point of this departure for, once again, there was no fingerpost or marker. Finally I found a stile, buried deep in a blackthorn, holly and hawthorn hedge (all the most hostile plants, I noted) and tangled about with brambles as thick as my thumb. The stile, at the back of the hedge, was thus totally inaccessible, the hedge had no gaps or holes in it and I wasn't about to get torn to pieces for the doubtful privilege of becoming lost again in the terrain beyond. So I continued along the road, hammering my hot and aching feet on the tarmac. There was clearly a campaign hereabouts to discourage the use of footpaths.

By noon I was boiling in full sun, on a hot road and approaching spot height 194. Rather than unshouldering my rucksack to find my hat, I unshipped the brolly - not against the rain this time but as a sunshade. At last a gap in the hedge enabled me to see the distant misty prospect of Llandovery in the valley below. After all those days of grey overcast and mist when I was longing for the sun to shine, here I was now seeking shade by using the umbrella. Towards noon I was passed by the first car I'd seen for two hours and the driver, in what seemed to be the local habit, gave me a wave. A decent local custom was that, acknowledging the presence of a walker. In Hereford one gets mouthed obscenities, rude gesticulations, close-shaving and hooting and generally one is treated as a form of inconvenient lowlife.

The descent down the lane towards Llandovery seemed endless and was made the more tiresome by the sun, which at first I welcomed but which now had become unsufferably hot. Thank God for the brolly. However my trial did eventually come to an end, for by half-twelve I was on the bridge* over the Towy which was a suspension bridge in Borrow's time but is now an

128

ugly structure of braced steel tubes. The river ran quietly and serenely below, keeping its air of timeless calm in the presence of the lorries thundering across the bridge on the A40, the arterial road link to west Wales. The outskirts of the town were not very charming. I strode past the conventional rows of Victorian semis, deluged by the roar and tumult of constant heavy traffic. What a nightmare after the peace and calm of the countryside from Caio. At the level crossing over the Heart of Wales railway line I paused for a bit to take in the railway ambience and idly noticed that some of the rail shoes were dated 1948 and held the rail in place by means of wooden wedges! Hardly suitable for modern, high-speed trains.   I realised that this was the only standard -gauge railway line that I had crossed in the whole walk.

I had a room booked at the Castle Hotel*, where Borrow had stayed, but was rather dismayed to find that the only single room they had looked onto the main road where heavy trucks carrying tree trunks, hay bales, farm machinery and the usual supermarket goods heaved past only ten feet from my window.

I'd arrived by lunchtime which left me the afternoon free to see if Borrow's description of the town was still in any way apt. In chapter 97 of 'Wild Wales' he wrote:

"Llandovery is a small but beautiful town, situated amidst fertile meadows. It is a water-girdled spot, whence its name Llanymddyfri, which signifies the church surrounded by water. The most striking object which Llandovery can show is its castle, from which the inn, which stands near to it, has its name. The castle, majestic though in ruins, stands on a green mound. It was one of the many strongholds of Griffith ap Nicholas, Lord of Dinevor." Borrow   devoted two pages of *Wild Wales* to this remarkable man. He then visited the church and expounds at length about Rees Pritchard, the much-revered vicar there about 1600. At the time of Borrow's visit in 1854 Rees Pritchard was still known as 'The Vicar'. But Borrow's most oft quoted accolade for Llandovery is: "Llandovery, I have no hesitation in saying, is about the pleasantest little town in which I have halted in the course of my wanderings".

I felt that this description was still largely appropriate today for the town has a neat and prosperous air. The town's showpiece is the cobbled market square, set back from the A40 and therefore away from the through-traffic. This attractive spot was neat, clean and well-maintained with freshly-painted ironwork, Edwardian style seats, bollards, lamp-posts and railings. The square was enclosed by handsome period houses in good decorative order. The post office was painted a subdued grey with turquoise trim around the windows; the hair salon was in pale orange with primrose yellow quoins at the corners offset by window boxes brimming with bright vermilion and purple petunias. The Jacobean town house painted terracotta with blue and white woodwork and white cornerstones was "The Drovers" bed and breakfast; Phillips' Antiques, of roughly the same age, was an intriguing building in that it had three dormer windows in the roof with triangular glazing and carved fascia boards. The shop was pale yellow with dark green cornerstones. The pubs in the centre were dark and cool with an interesting range of ales. The Bear Inn was also terracotta, neat and trim with gleaming, freshly cleaned window glass. The Hongkong and Shanghai Banking Corporation was in cream and brown with a porticoed door and Georgian sash windows. The centre of the square featured a fountain in marble, or pseudo-marble, dedicated to Dr Frederick William Lewis 1851-1899. All in all the square was a fresh and colourful place to sit and relax. The Castle Hotel was resplendent with hanging baskets and window boxes of brilliant flowers; the ruined castle still stands on its 'green mound' though the historical ambience is damaged by the huge car park in front.

Notwithstanding all these charms, the town is made noisy, smelly and ugly by the constant passage, right through its centre, of heavy lorries. What a shame that this charming little town has to suffer this wheelborne violation, day in, day out.

The information board in the car park gave a potted history of the town. *"Llandovery's position at the junction of ancient routes linking Dyfed with Powys led to its growth as a strategic military centre. In the first century the Romans built a fort here. The first motte and bailey castle was built of wood by the Normans around 1100 which was a far-flung outpost and vulnerable to attack. By 1162 the castle was in the hands of Rhys ap Griffith a local lord. It fell to the English in 1277 and was held until 1490 when it was abandoned and fell into disrepair. During Owain Glyndwr's war of liberation in the early 1400s, Henry the Fourth led a huge army through the town in search of Glyndwr. Llewellyn ap Griffith* (who was apparently born at Caio), *a supporter of Glyndwr, was publicly hung, drawn and quartered in 1401 because he refused to betray his master and the cause of Welsh freedom. His sacrifice is marked by the memorial sculpture, in bright stainless steel, on the castle mound next to the ruins of the castle tower"*.

From the castle mound I could see the whole of the town and out to the hilly country beyond. For me, in a town, it is always reassuring to be able to see open countryside. The impression of the town is one of brightly painted period buildings for the most part but of course inevitably fouled-up by some modern monsters the most tragic of which is the Town and Country Stores' great, grey, steel-clad warehouse immediately below the castle. As I returned towards the hotel I encountered a group of elderly folk, dressed as if for a funeral, who were conducting an animated conversation in Welsh, not a word of which could I understand. I returned to my room, just outside which the endless stream of lorries was still thundering. The hotel was sadly positioned at a narrowing in the road, or rather its position had caused the narrowing in the road, which forced these huge trucks even closer to my bed.

To escape this I went to wander round the hotel interior. It was unmodernised and fitted with aged wall panelling, bent oak beams, inglenook fireplaces and dark-stained, small windows: all very redolent of a bygone age. In the lounge I found enormous sagging armchairs and thick Axminster carpets under the low ceilings and a party, possibly a wedding party, singing songs in Welsh. In the foyer a pinboard held a collection of testimonials from satisfied guests and a letter referring to the 'Borrow Bed'.

Aha, so some smart-alec had identified the bed that he'd slept in, which amazingly, was still in the hotel after 150 years and had made an attempt to establish its provenance. It seemed that the so-called 'Borrow Bed' was mid nineteenth century and possibly (only possibly, mind) made before his stay in 1854. It is a 'half-tester' pattern with an unusual footboard and was possibly made by John Davies of Carmarthen. The bed was evidently now used as a tourist attraction for one could sleep in it, in the same room that it always had been.

Before finding a pub for my supper I bought some earplugs in the chemist shop for I had a feeling that I'd be needing them to sleep at all in that room.

***

Some useful translations.

Gwyn	white
Goch or coch	red
Glas	blue
Ddu	black
Gwyrdd	green
Llwyd	grey

Shwmae	hello
Bore da	good morning
Nos da	good night
Hwyl fawr	goodbye
Iechyd da	good health

The Castle Hotel at Llandovery

Memorial to Llewellyn ap Griffith at Llandovery

The hills ahead

First view of Swansea Bay

Eleventh day

OVER THE CULTURAL DIVIDE

Well, I slept until about six when even the earplugs could not block out the racket of the early morning lorries. The pleasant old-fashioned ambience of the hotel was not reflected in a pleasant breakfast, old-fashioned, or otherwise. I simply cannot understand why it is, in this age of dietary enlightenment, that hotels persist in serving the same boring, stodgy fare of the full British breakfast: the solid eggs, the soggy tomatoes, the tasteless dry sausage, the dessicated microwaved beans, the greasy fried bread, the anaemic white toast, the bitter coffee. I'd had wonderful fresh, healthy breakfasts containing not one of these ingredients at guest houses charging half of this hotel's tariff.

After the unappetising meal, I sat outside to lace my boots, amused by the cursing of the man who was entangled in the hose with which he was trying to water the hanging baskets and window boxes on the front facade of the hotel.

Borrow intended to spend his next night at a place he calls Gutter Vawr in the county of Glamorgan. There is no place of that name these days but it appears from study of his text that it was at, or near, the present town of Brynamman. His account of the day's walk is very vague as to place names and the actual route that he followed. From his text I could only cull the following clues.

"Crossing a bridge over the Bran just before it enters the greater stream, I proceeded along a road running nearly south with a fine range of hills on the east. In about an hour I reached Llangadog. Leaving Llangadog I pushed forward. In two or three hours *(how vague can you be George?)* I came to a glen, the sides of which were beautifully wooded.The river, I was told by a lad, was the Sawdde. Passed a pretty village on my right in the shape of a semicircle and in about half an hour came to a bridge over a river which I supposed to be the Sawdde which I had already seen, but which I subsequently learned was a different stream. It was running from the south. After some time *(Didn't Borrow have a pocket-watch?)* I reached another bridge at the foot of a lofty ascent."

Because Borrow was following the Sawdde river he must have been on the line of the modern A4069. As he is so vague as to the times elapsed, it is difficult to be sure, but the "semi-circular pretty village was probably Pont ar Llechan and the bridge he crossed half-an-hour later was Pont Newydd but the river under the bridge was the Clydach whose confluence with the Sawdde he had not seen just before the bridge. His next bridge "after some time" could have been Pont Aber, which does indeed have some steep slopes to the west and south, but, equally, it could have been Pont Flocksman. When Borrow asked "a decent-looking man sawing a piece of wood" what was the name of the river that he'd left about a mile behind him, he was told that the river was the Lleidach, certainly the modern Clydach so he was still on the A4069.

After some conversation with this man Borrow went on his way. "The road led in a south-eastern direction gradually upwards to very lofty regions." He then had an encounter with some Romany folk and enquired about Jasper Petulengro. (A bit far-fetched this, for Petulengro is the main character in Borrow's book 'Romany Rye' and it is not clear whether he was fictitious or real). In due course Borrow came to Capel Gwynfa.

This part of his narrative makes no geographical sense as the A4069 does indeed lead up to "very lofty regions" but Capel Gwynfa, which he did arrive at, is about a kilometre to the west of the A4069 and not loftily above it. To reach the village he would have had to cross the Clydach river via a considerable detour and then return to the main road. That he was still on the line of the A4069 is confirmed by his next landmark, which was a toll-gate called Cowslip Gate because toll-gates would only have existed on the main roads. His route from Capel Gwynfa to Gutter Fawr, or Brynamman, is impossible to determine but it's likely that he followed the A4069 all the way.

134

He proceeded into the misty night and at length he "gained the top". Here, he says, "the road turned and made a steep descent towards the south-west. He saw a "frightful precipice" on his left and heard "every now and then loud noises in the vale probably proceeding from stone quarries." Later he noticed "blazes down below, resembing those of furnaces", crossed "a bridge over a kind of torrent" and arrived at "the tavern of Gutter Vawr in the county of Glamorgan."

Borrow nowhere mentions the name of this tavern. Assuming that Gutter Vawr is the present-day Brynamman, one cannot be sure of where he stayed because there are only two inns, or pubs, now in the town of Brynamman. One, the Derlwyn Arms does not offer accommodation; the other, the Tregib Arms, does.

He doubtless followed the line of the A4069 to Llangadoc and from there his route took him up the Sawdde valley, probably again on the main road, and to Capel Gwynfa. After that his description is too vague to be certain of his route although there were many quarries either side of the A4069 as it crosses The Black Mountain and his "blazes down below" could have the ironworks in the valley at Brynamman

I, once again, decided that I would not follow the main road to the Sawdde valley but take a more interesting and less dangerous and noisy route to the Sawdde, then to Pont ar Llechan, which I'm fairly sure Borrow passed and, by lanes, to Capel Gwynfa. From there I'd take tracks and bridlepaths over the mountain to Brynamman.

Ths sun was coming up behind the castle in Llandovery as I left the town. I crossed the river Bran and turned up the lane to Myddfai, walking directly into glorious rising sunshine. The gentle meadows and hills were incandescent with dew; sparkling light pervaded the morning.The hedgerow leaves shivered in the slight breeze to shed their drops of moisture on my boots. As I began to ascend the long climb up out of the Tywi valley I faintly heard the clickety-clack of a train approaching Llandovery station. Had Borrow heard the same I wondered. It is doubtful that the railway was there as early as 1854. He was not fond of railways and perhaps that explains why he never mentioned them in his text.

There was little else to hear in the quiet of the early morning save the rushing of streams and the gurgle of water in the roadside drains. I passed a Forestry Commission plantation where a green sign proudly announced that its name was "Llwyn-y-Wormwood". What a strange mix of Welsh and English, and this was the second time I'd come across 'wormwood'. Why hadn't the FC called it "Llwyn-y-Chwerwlys"? Probably because the last part would be unpronounceable for those not speaking Welsh.

There were some steep little ascents, as shown by the arrowheads on the map. I wondered if the weather would change during the day for I had the pleasure of listening to the distant, warbling song of a mistle-thrush, the storm cock, whose song is supposed to presage bad weather. This sound brought to mind all of the poem 'The Darkling Thrush' by Thomas Hardy but in particular the last verse:

"So little cause for carolings
    of such ecstatic sound
was written on terrestrial things
    afar or nigh around,
that I could think there trembled through
    his happy goodnight air
some blessed Hope, whereof he knew
    and I was unaware"

The mournful song of a robin and the deep, liquid twerp-twerp-twerp of a nuthatch entertained me further as I sweated along in the sun and the dew. As I came to the first rise on the lane I was treated to a glorious view of the misty, glittering hill ridge of this western end of The Black Mountain, far off as yet, but enticing, alluring and entirely tranquil. The road dropped as far as the bridge over the Afon Ydw and then abruptly went uphill again. Oh, dear, another switchback day! By nine I crossed

136

into the Brecon Beacons National Park (now known as 'Bannau Brycheiniog') at a cross-roads where the road levelled off. I'd been troubled only by two school buses, and no other traffic; this kind of road walking was really no more unpleasant than footpath walking except that it was harder underfoot. I was hoping, of course, that now I was in the National Park the paths would be better signposted and better maintained than the rubbish I'd had to cope with recently. Well, this was not to be.

It was a calm landscape of gently sloping pasture land well-filled with sheep who seemed to have also caught the dew. The trees in the copses and hedgerows broke up the fields into a pleasing, and apparently random, pattern of short and tall, dark and light, soft and harsh. Myddfai village was a pretty little place; well cared-for, clean and neat, a chapel deep in a froth of meadowsweet, a pub with no litter. The three miles from Llandovery had taken me exactly an hour. Having passed through the village I realised that, once again, I'd seen no-one to speak to. I had passed a man wiping dew off his wing-mirrors in the village but he looked so disreputable that I thought I wouldn't risk a conversation. Beyond Myddfai I walked on into the golden morning; the pleasing mixed landscape on my left was put into low-relief by the ridge of the hills behind: To my right the valley of the Afon Bran (another one) was made mysterious by a swaddling of mist but the forest of Cilgwyn Wood was brightly lit by the sun. A venerable and aged oak startled me by suddenly coming to life with a clashing of twigs and a bashing of leaves; two squirrels were foraging for acorns and clambering away out of my sight.

At half-nine I turned off the road onto a track which, according to the map, led to a homestead called Cwm Bran. This was tarmac to begin, but so covered in decades of mud and dung that it was difficult to tell. Beyond a summit the track became grassy and boggy, and led downhill into the Bran valley. The track ended abruptly at Troed y Rhiw and so I had to climb a gate and traverse a field or two before crossing a bridge where the map showed a ford. The farm of Cwm Bran featured a vast concrete farmyard, immaculately clean, containing the weird tableau of thirteen immobile cats and a man pushing a wheelbarrow full of what appeared to be dead chickens. The public footpath through and beyond the farm was not marked on the ground or signposted. Why was I not surprised? But the line was clear enough on the map so I marched on with confidence following the hedge through damp river meadows. Where the right-of-way came to the edge of Coed Deri, there was no stile, no gate, no means of crossing the ugly tangle of netting and barbed wire and, as far as I could see, no means of penetrating the dense woodland itself.

I had no choice but to follow the edge of the wood in a southerly direction, which was the way I wanted to go anyway. After ten minutes the wood had narrowed to a strip and I thought I'd better cross it to get to the footpath on the other side. A mighty struggle ensued; the wood contained a deep-cut stream whose banks were steep, loose, and infested with man-eating brambles. The path, when I finally reached it in a rather bloodied state, led me to Coed Weddus farm where I could not find the path that led due south. There were no finger posts or waymarkers. I was standing in a field next to the farm bungalow, scratching my head and unshipping my rucksack to get my compass when a voice asked: "Can I help you?". I explained my problem and the young woman directed me back and onto the path leading west where I was to look for a stile, which she called a stylus. Before leaving I asked her if the name 'Gutter Vawr' meant anything to her. After a pause she said: "No, it doesn't. Could it be Goytre Fawr that you're headed for?" Well this was a thought, certainly, and it is possible that Borrow's Gutter Vawr was an Anglicised version of this. Anyway, it was no help, so I thanked her and went to look for the 'stylus'. I found it eventually, after several minutes search, buried deep in a hedge and invisible if one didn't know it was there.

A stroll across fields with cows brought me to the lane at Rhiwiau Isaf. I suffered some serious dog trouble there. As I passed the farmhouse, walking on a public road and minding my own business, four dogs came bounding out of the house, barking and snarling. One leapt the wall and approached me in a boisterous, not to say aggressive, manner so I told it to clear off and leave me alone. A woman then appeared in the front yard of the house and shouts, as dog owners always do, "They don't mean you any harm." I said, as I always do, "You know that, but I don't. They certainly don't look harmless to me. Get them under control." She said, "Don't be so aggressive." I replied, " You teach your dogs to be less aggressive to harmless walkers." Her response was: "Don't be so stupid." Well, I was now losing my temper and retorted "Look, here am I walking up this road minding my own business and I'm now being chased up a public highway by your dogs.It's a bloody disgrace."

I marched off in high dudgeon and promptly took a wrong turning on the road and had to toil back uphill for 300 metres to find the right one. Blasted dogs. Silly woman. By eleven I was on the lane above Caeaubychain Bach (there's a mouthful for the Saxon!) whence I had a fine elevated view of Llangadoc spread in the valley below. Directly ahead I could see a distinctive, bare, russet-coloured hill that stood out from the surrounding scenery not merely because of its height but because it was devoid of green vegetation. And just behind it to the right was another, smaller hill of the same type. These were incongruous features in this lushly green and gentle landscape, especially as there seemed to be some kind of rampart round the hilltop.The map showed them to be two fortified hilltops called Y Gaer Fawr and Y Gaer Fach on a chunk of rising ground, called Carn Goch, on the hillside that sloped down to the Towy valley. What magnificent defensive positions these must have been with extensive views up and down the valley.

Where the road abruptly turned left to enter the Sawdde valley; the landscape changed abruptly too. From soft and gentle farmland I walked into a coniferous landscape where the entire hillside beyond was one huge evergreen plantation. I walked into conifers on this side too where the road entered a dark and sunless trench among the trees. Beyond this stern and forbidding foreground, up the valley, rose the big hills of The Black Mountain. Crikey, was I going up there?

But for now the road led down towards the sounding cataract of the river and a right hand turn over a bridge and into the tiny hamlet of Pont ar Llechau*. The river rushed noisily over its rocky bed below the bridge; more white water than clear water. It was the verticality of the red sandstone strata in the river bed that created the rapids. At the hamlet, only one person was in sight and he was on a roof doing something tricky with what looked like a large snake. I hurried across the main road here, the A4069, past the former pub whose decrepit sign of three horseshoes was still, but only just, suspended on the gable wall. There were perhaps half a dozen stone houses here. Someone, notwithstanding the rather traffic-noisy and tree-gloomy situation, had built a new bungalow opposite an unusual circular stone edifice full of firewood logs.

I took the lane opposite, signposted Gwynfa, and began the second uphill grind of the day. To amuse myself whilst so doing I intended to note how many of the footpaths leading off this road actually had fingerposts. The one leading to Bailey Home Farm didn't. I had to pause to admire the spectacular view of the Bannau Sir Gaer above Llyn y Fan Fach which I'd never seen from this angle before. It seemed very high in the blue sky of that sunny morning, like the leading prow of the ship that consisted of the other summits of The Black Mountain, behind it. It did look very inviting, clear, calm and peaceful.

The next footpath at a small wood, did have a finger post but the following one, at the wood's far corner, didn't. I could have taken this as a short cut to Gwynfa, but didn't for I could see fallen trees, brambles, reeds and lots of other rebarbative vegetation. The next footpath wasn't signed. As I approached the cross roads at Bryn Clydach I spied two sheepdogs lurking furtively at the farm gate, as they do, and prepared myself for more dog bother. False alarm it was, as they both utterly ignored me. Unpredictable, are dogs.

My first impression of Capel Gwynfa* was of a 1960s bunglow, grey gable ends, scaffolding and tin sheds. A footpath fingerpost; a carved village sign; some privatised council houses; a newly-built chapel (truly a rare sight!); a pair of eagles carved into a dead tree trunk; a disused chapel; a large church with a top-heavy tower and ugly gargoyles; a Wincanton articulated lorry; and finally a white mansion were the notable landmarks as I completed my traverse of the village. Not much there then, and certainly nothing that might at one time have been an inn. Borrow had commented on the steepness of the road leaving Pont ar Llechau and, arriving at Capel Gwynfa, he wrote: "I came to a little village, consisting of three or four houses: one of them, at the door of which several carts were standing, bore the sign of a tavern." He obtained the name of the place of a man who was breaking stones on the road.

The public footpath at the end of the village had no fingerpost, nor did the next path on the right. I was aiming for the village school, about a kilometre beyond the village, where I hoped to take a footpath southwards towards the mountain.

The school, although no longer one, was immediately identifiable by its typical village-school architecture. There was no fingerpost here and the alleyway beside the school was not obviously the footpath but I took it anyway, found a fingerpost a few metres in and then fought through weeds and nettles to a gate and open fields. Feeling that I was not on a right-of-way, I crossed a couple of fields, got onto a foully muddy track and crossed the Nant Toddeb. From here the public right of way track led southwards for about two kilometres. The going was muddy and dungy and under water in some places. There had clearly been much tractor and cattle traffic here. I got pretty filthy. But the hills were drawing closer and it wasn't long before the route changed its character to a pleasant, sunken green lane, rocky underfoot. The hedges either side were plainly very ancient judging by the massive girth of the pleached stems and the profusion of different species. An old drovers' road, perhaps.

Just before one o'clock I came to the end of the track and a gate out onto the open hillside. The right of way shown on the map ascended the slope in a rather peculiar shape of irregular zig-zags. On the ground I soon found that this line was deeply eroded, in fact it was now a water-course. As water would never have naturally followed a line like this, I concluded that it was an ancient route up the hill and, deeply eroded by centuries of use, had become a stream. Man zig-zags uphill, water doesn't zig-zag downhill. This was steep, sweat-pumping, heart-thumping work through typical moorland terrain of poor grass, gorse, bracken and reedy bits. I reached the mountain road at Clogau Bach at a height of 386 metres with a gasp and great relief.   A group of wild ponies were grazing here, eyeing me suspiciously and swishing their tails at the plaguing flies.

Borrow's route from Capel Gwynfa is very hard to determine. "Presently", *(yes, yes, yes but how long was that exactly, George?)* "I came to a little cottage with a toll-bar. Seeing a woman standing at the door I inquired of her the name of the gate."
"Cowslip Gate, sir."
"Has it any Welsh name?"
"None that I know of, sir.""
There is no trace of a place of this name today but the presence of a toll-gate suggests that he was walking on the main highway of the time, a line that is certainly the same as that of the A4069. However, Cowslip Gate was, to quote Borrow, "at a considerable altitude, and commanded an extensive view to the south, west, and north." He went to the south for a little way on the level; the road then turned abruptly to the east and became steep. He then writes: "After the turn, I had a huge chalk cliff towering over me on the right and a chalk precipice on my left." Borrow was evidently no geologist for there is no chalk hereabouts but plenty of light-coloured limestone.

Having reached the mountain road, which ran east to west, I turned west and enjoyed walking on the level for a kilometre or

142

so. This gave me a chance to inspect the bizarre landscape above the road. The hillside was broken with tiers of harsh crags, limestone outcrops and the vegetated spoil-heaps of old quarry workings. It was disconcerting to suddenly come upon this industrial waste landscape up there in the hills, set in sharp contrast to the green beauty of the country below. Did I say limestone? Hum, well there was red sandstone just down there in that eroded zig-zag path gully. It seemed that this narrow strip of tarmac marked the junction of two bedrock types, quite abruptly. The map showed disused quarries, so that accounted man's imprint on the terrain and, a little further south, shake holes (or 'sink-holes'), so that confirmed the limestone. There was nothing to be heard save the faint mewing of a buzzard and the soughing of the wind in the reeds and grasses and through the dismal crags.

Where the road bent south to cross the upper reaches of the Nant Oesglyn I took a rest, around one o'clock, out of the breeze, sitting on the culvert with my feet skimming the stream waters. I'd seen very little traffic all day, but whilst I sat and chewed, first an aged rocker hummed past on a vintage Triumph, then an open-top MG TF racketed round the bend soon to be followed by a middle-aged man with a pigtail peacefully riding a tricycle. Well, what unexpected antiquery! And how extraordinary. Was there some kind of veteran rally on somewhere? I enjoyed the view to the north. I could clearly see Capel Gwynfe far below and away to the right, the deep gash of the Sawdde valley and the massive forest on its left bank.

My objective now was the bridle path which led over the mountain, more or less parallel with the A4069. Perhaps this had been Borrow's route after all? But no, there wouln't have been a toll-gate on a drovers' road, surely? Having further pondered this conundrum, and now rested, I took a short cut and attained this well-marked route where it crossed a spur. I could now look elsewhere than at my feet, for the going was easy underfoot and something made me look up. Almost immediately overhead two red kites were soaring, silently, smoothly but then, seeing me, they swept away downwind. Magnificent birds, and the first I'd seen this far south. And then ahead, two more came into view and suddenly there were six of them, flying in pairs at different heights easily identifiable by their forked tails. Eight red kites! What a treat! I stood and admired their mastery of the air until they all disappeared downwind.

The track became less well-defined as I gained height towards the ridge but, as I neared the skyline, the line of the route became marked by parallel lines of boulders, about twenty feet apart, on either side, almost a pair of ruined walls. These were a distinct linear feature, between which the track ran, obviously man-made and presumably intended to mark the line of the route so that drovers wouldn't lose it in mist, and to contain their cattle. It was probably never used by wheeled vehicles for the ground was bouldery from time to time with some steep little drops. Yes, an ancient drovers' road, I guessed between the industrial area of Swansea and the agricultural land of the Towy valley.

I paused on the high point, looked ahead and saw.........the sea! Swansea Bay, at last. Menai Strait to Swansea Bay! From sea to shining sea. And beyond the silver-gleam of the bay, the Bristol Channel and dimly, far beyond, the purple blur of the coast of North Devon. And looking right the rugged peninsula of Gower floated on a glittering sea and beyond, just visible as a smudge, what could have been Caldey Island. A staggering view, all the more astonishing for being totally unexpected. A fantastic panorama extending for about 50 or 60 miles. What a treat; what a day! The descending ridge off to the west was a rust-brown blanket of expired heather, oddly speckled with white limestone boulders. Before me the land dipped down into the valley where lay Brynamman, beyond which the land rose again, the last range of hills before Swansea, the hills that I would cross tomorrow. It was warm now, in the sunshine, in the gentle zephyrs, so I sat for a while to enjoy the amazing view and take some photos.

The track led easily downhill for some time before the two lines of marker boulders gradually petered out. Then, on softer rock, the route became deeply eroded, attracted surface-water and became a water-course containing a wide ribbon of reeds and marsh grass. I lost it altogether at the edge of a vast area of marsh which I had to cross to stay on the west side of the stream gully leading into Brynamman. Stopping for a moment to gather my strength for the wet struggle ahead, I looked east. The main road was clearly visible and there a tourist coach was parked close to a disused quarry which was also plain to see. The peculiar thing was that, in the quarry, about 30 people were doing God knows what: some were standing about, some were bent over and some were half-way up the quarry face. I watched for a while to see if I could work out what they were up to and eventually decided that they must have been on some geology field trip.

The map showed a huge area of opencast mining on the hill just beyond Brynamman, which I was now looking directly at but most of it seemed to have been filled in, reclaimed for grazing for the hillside was unnaturally green and smooth. A black hole was, however, visible over the foreground ridge of this worked terrain, so perhaps some opencasting still went on. The marsh, really an ankle-deep lake with tussocks of red-seeded grasses and reeds was exceedingly foul and hard work for quarter of an hour. I soon wished I'd made a detour to avoid it.

Finally, the exit from the moor and from the Brecon Beacons National Park back into farmland was a gate with a fingerpost. A notice board here, at the gate, bore the message:

"This area of open hill is valued for its upland landscape ecology, its many archaeological features and wilderness qualities. Much of the 15 000 hectares has been recognised as an SSSI. The common is grazed by livestock from local farms. Please try not to disturb flocks away from their natural grazing area. The common is owned and managed by the Brecon Beacons National Park for the purposes of conserving the landscape and providing for its quiet enjoyment."

Immediately adjacent to this proud statement of environmental rectitude, an appalling litter of agricultural ugliness greeted me as I stepped through the gate and onto the lane. Rusting railway wagons, mountains of black-clad silage, rotting metal-clad barns, green-stained cinder-block walls, weed-infested redundant machinery and a mobile phone mast welcomed me back from the purity of the hills.

"The world is too much with us; late and soon,
   getting and spending, we lay waste our powers;
   little we see in Nature that is ours;
we have given our hearts away, a sordid boon!"
(William Wordsworth)

As I came down the lane towards the outskirts of Brynamman it was clearly obvious that I was now in a South Wales valley environment; that I had crossed the cultural divide, represented by the geographical watershed, from agrarian mid-Wales to the industrial south. The approach to the valley town was typical: a scattering of down-at-heel homesteads with mouldy walls, corrugated iron and irregular fences on the higher land; lower down a denser grouping of unattractive modern bungalows, for the land is cheap, aspiring to be desirable detached residences; and at the edge of the town the steep terraces of Victorian villas whose dilapidated fronts looked out onto broken pavements and a pot-holed street.

I passed a front hedge, badly butchered, whose mangled branches lay in a chaotic mess, just as they'd fallen. I chuckled at the sight of a neat and tidy detached house, modernised, but with an apparently still operative earth closet in the garden. I wrinkled my nose in disgust at a huge pile of farmyard manure steaming in the front garden of a badly modernised stone cottage. I walked to the ever-present sound of running water and barking dogs, down towards the narrow, noisy and congested valley streets. By three-thirty I was back in the ugly man-built environment of an industrial valley town. Here the accents were different; the people had a resigned, but cheerful, air; everyone was, however,

146

very friendly. I had no difficulty finding folk to talk to, nor in getting help, directions, information or advice.

George Borrow, on arrival at Gutter Vawr, partook of a veal and bacon supper amid the prodigious noise of miners and carters making merry. Of the kitchen, he wrote: "It was nearly filled with rough, unkempt fellows smoking, drinking, whistling, singing, shouting or jabbering, some in a standing, some in a sitting posture." He subsequently had some conversation with the denizens about why they fell silent on his entry, about the Crimean War, about Russia, Turkey and Spain. Before going to bed Borrow told the assembled drinkers a ghost story that he learnt in Spain, Lope de Vega's ghost story, which he considered "decidedly the best ghost story in the world".

***

Translations of some common nouns used in the text

Afon	river
Bryn	hill
Bwlch	pass or col
Caer	fortress
Castell	castle
Coed	wood or forest
Drws	doorway, gateway, gap
Groes	cross
Maen	rock or stone
Mynydd	mountain
Pen	head or top
Pont	bridge
Rhos	moor or common
Rhyd	ford
Waun	flat, grassy plain

FROM MINING TO MOTORWAY

Gutter Fawr, or Brynamman, was evidently a mining town in 1854 as Borrow's view from his bedroom window testified. "Immediately beyond a roaring brook was a bank, not of green turf, grey rock or brown mould, but of coal rubbish, coke and cinders: on the top of this bank was a fellow performing some dirty office or other, with a spade and barrow: beyond him, on the other side of a hill, was a tramway, up which a horse was straining, drawing a load of something towards the north-west. Beyond the tramway was a grove of yellow-looking firs: beyond the firs a range of white houses with blue roofs, occupied, I suppose, by miners and their families; and beyond these I caught sight of the mountain on the top of which I had been the night before, only a partial one, however, as large masses of mist were still hanging about it. The morning was moist and dripping, and nothing could look more cheerless and uncomfortable than the entire scene."

Well, he was obviously not impressed and although the mining detritus is no longer there, the place still has a grubby and depressing atmosphere.

He thought he should visit the local iron foundry and saw " a large steam engine at full play, terrible furnaces, and immense heaps of burning, crackling cinders, and a fiery stream of molten metal rolling along." He was told that no English or Irish worked on the premises; all workers were Welsh. He then set off for Swansea, about thirteen miles away. He didn't like the country for the first few miles because " it consisted of low, sullen peaty hills." It improved later and became "bold, wild and pleasantly wooded." In his text he then proffers a translation of Ap Gwilym's ode to the sun and Glamorgan.

After an unspecified time he "came to Llanguick, a hamlet situated near a tremendous gorge, the sides of which were covered with wood. Thence to the village of Tawy Bridge." Later he came to Mr Pearson's ironworks and fell in with another walker. Their conversation occupies four pages of the book before their ways parted. Borrow arrived at a place called Glandwr, about two miles from Swansea, where he entered an inn and, for sixpence, had a glass of ale, a boot polish and a clothes wipe and brush because he wanted to look smart to enter the big city. Chapter 100 of "Wild Wales' ends with: "Presently I entered the town, a large, bustling, dirty, gloomy place, and inquiring for the first hotel was directed to the Mackworth Arms in Wine Street."

From this it is, again, difficult to determine what was Borrow's route for the day. His descriptive narrative of the day's walking is very thin, not to say sparse and give very few clues as to his route or what he saw. Indeed most of Chapters 99,100 and 101 in Wild Wales consist of the conversational dialogue he had with sundry innkeepers, drinkers and passers-by. It is probable that he, as usual, followed the line of our modern main roads. From Brynamman he could have taken the A474 through Gwaun Cae Gurwen and Cwmgorse to Pontardawe (the Bridge on the Tawe, or what Borrow called Tawy Bridge). One doubts that he went over the hills for that would have been mentioned in his narrative, I'm sure. However, as he mentions Llanguick which is conceivably the present-day Llangiwg, or Craig Llangiwg, which lies to the north-east of Pontardawe, it is more likely that he took the A4068 to Gurnos, then the A4067 past Llangiwg to Pontardawe.

I thought long and hard about my route for this day. I didn't want to spend the last day of a great walk toiling through noisy and ugly valley towns: I wanted to stay as high and remote as possible for as long as possible. As it turned out, I managed to do so. I perused the maps at great length. Eventually I decided that the great man had got this day all wrong. I would go west from Brynamman, following the Aman river until I could cross the A474 and get onto high ground over Mynydd y Gwair. A complex route would then lead me to junction 46 of the M4 where I would end my walk at the pub at Llangyfelach. There seemed no point in going further; no point in degrading the walk by flogging across suburban Swansea.

Brynamman was a singularly unprepossessing place with no merit at all that I could see. The narrow and tortuous main road through the town was clogged with traffic, heavy lorries struggling to negotiate the hairpin bends in the centre and fighting for space with taxis, buses and cars.

Relieved to quit this sink of noise and fumes I left the post office at nine o'clock, in a westerly direction through very unattractive streets where the housing consisted of modern infill between typical, older valleys' terraces. Where the street bore sharply right I took, against my better judgement, a footpath which followed the river more closely than the indirect road alternative.The grass wasn't too long for cows were grazing. At the end of the second field I crossed a stile into an area of scrubland with a gravel track leading south - this wasn't farmland. A glance at the map showed this to be the access road to an area of spoil heaps labelled 'Tip'. Hum, this didn't look too promising. But lo!, what's this, an information board? I read:

"Ynys Dawela Nature Park is owned by Carmarthenshire County Council and managed by the Countryside Recreation Section with assistance from the Friends of Ynys Dawela, a local volunteer group. The park was bought from the British Coal Board by the former Dinefor Borough Council in 1995 when plans for opencast mining on the site were abandoned. It has since been developed for quiet recreation and educational use. The park covers an area of 39 acres, and was originally farmland. A network of footpaths round the site gives easy access to flower-rich meadows , riverside and woodlands. The site has a history of coal mining and the south-western side is predominantly covered by a layer of washery waste from this period. It is now densely overgrown with gorse, birch and broom which will, over the years, improve the soil for other tree species. This area of coal-mining waste provides a contrast with the old agricultural land, not only in its general appearance but also in terms of the plant and animal species that it supports.

The park is situated on the northern side of the Aman valley with its northern boundary running adjacent to the Brecon Beacons National Park and its southern boundary is the fast-flowing and beautiful river Aman."

Well, that's all fine, but where are the footpath markers for me to follow my chosen route? I took the only road possible, down the gravel track which led through scrub to an open area with a hut or two and some tables. The exit route from this was not obvious nor signposted A tortuous path led me through a dense jungle of exactly what was mentioned on the info board. It was very quiet and calm amongst the gorse, birch and broom there in the early morning dew-damp and it became wetter underfoot as I descended along a well-defined path towards the river. I followed the path along the river bank through patchy woodland and then a soggy meadow but eventually the path came to a dead end against wire fencing. The river, running clear and shallow on a stony bed, was too deep to cross dry-shod so I had to turn back for about 500 metres until I found a muddy track leading uphill. At the edge of the scrubland I climbed a gate into a field and turned left towards some rooftops which I reasoned must be on the road at Tir Syr Walter. At a back garden I stopped to ask a man in a garden if there was a footpath by here.

He replied: " Erm, oo, I dunno butt. Never seen no-one hiking by 'ere. Watchew dooin? "

I explained but without any perceptible effect. Hopeless.

Looking carefully ahead, I said, " Is that a stile over there?"

He replied, " Ooo, ah, yup, mebbe."

I'd decided that it was a stile, in the face of lack of local knowledge, but before I could leave he asked,

" Wanna sweet?".

Rather taken aback by this sudden show of hospitality, I agreed and he offered me two soggy boiled sweets in sticky paper.

"Ta, these'll wet my whistle", I grinned at him, said "Tara", and went on, vainly trying to unstick the two blobs of gunk from my fingers.

Some turns by back gardens led me to the lane where a finger post indicated a footpath but, once again, there had been no way markers across the meadow or through the Nature Park. Shortly I crossed the river bridge, went under a disused railway bridge, crossed a tributary of the Afon Amman and came out onto the main valley road. Almost opposite a signpost pointed the way up a steep lane to Bryncethin. As I toiled up the lane in the warm sunshine I fell into conversation with a local woman who said, "I can see your maps. Where are you going?"

I replied, "Llangyfelach is my destination today, and it's still a little way off!"

"Ooh, I never. Where is it then?"

"It's down by Swansea, on the motorway".

"Well, that is a long way. We used to do a lot of walking, mind, but Phillip's just been seriously ill so we don't anymore. But he's working on getting fit again."

I said, "Well, what about you?"

"Oh, I'll have to get on my bike again, I suppose".

"Why don't you walk up this hill with me? That'll clear some clogged arteries!"

She retorted, "Ooh no, I couldn't, I don't know you from Adam. Anyway, I walk up and down here everyday".

I sweated on, steeply up the lane where the housing stock improved in affluence as I ascended. These were certainly not underprivileged valley houses but large detached mansions set in their own grounds and with extensive views down into the Amman valley. It didn't take long to leave behind the scruffy confined streets of the valley. Near the end of the lane I took a signposted path to the right, crossed some sheep pasture and a fence and got onto open moorland. From here there were fine views of the valley and the route that I'd descended the previous day from The Black Mountain.

A little further on, at the highest point, I paused to work out my best route to Henrhyd. It was not obvious for the moor was featureless and the bridle path I intended to follow wasn't discernible. I decided that I was on Banc Cwmhelen, took a compass bearing on the path over Mynydd y Betws and walked on. The going was easy underfoot being dry, short grass. Keeping an eye on the only landmark - the radio mast to the west - I soon came across the bridleway. This led me south-west and downhill to the farm at Henrhyd.

This range of hills, though over 300 metres high, was about only three kilometres wide but the vast brown moor had the appearance of a much more extensive barrier. The black scar of an open-cast mine blotched the landscape to the south-east; attempts had obviously been made to convert as much of the moor to grazing land as possible for the field network extended higher than normal hereabouts. These meadows had been phosphated to an unlikely brilliant green which was made all the more incongruous by the interspersed patches of brown unimproved land. The illusion of wildness was further destroyed by the tyre tracks of off-road vehicles, the roar of the dragline in the opencast pit and the scream of a jet far above in the cerulean.

The homestead of Henrhyd was an ugly mess of inelegant buildings, tin roofed sheds, a stone barn with no roof, a neglected house with a double pitched roof and green-stained walls, a hideous clutter of ancient rusting ironwork. But for the presence of a car and a white van I would have thought that the place was uninhabited. This presumably former sheep farm, and the nearby overhead power lines, despoiled an otherwise pretty valley at the southern foot of Mynydd y Betws. But the kites evidently found it an agreeable spot for a pair was soaring in the thermals directly above the farm. They were very low, about the same height as the overhead cables and seemingly not disturbed by my presence as buzzards would have been.

The route now became a stony track, in fact the farm access track, going diagonally up the flank of the ridge that formed the west side of Cwm Clydach. This valley was pleasant enough, but not remarkable and my enjoyment of it was tainted by my awareness of the industrial landscape just over the hill. The ascending track, passing through typical Welsh moorland, came to a tarmac road which I crossed and continued up the same line on a grassy path. Unusually, there were cows grazing up there at over 300 metres where one would normally expect to see sheep. I caught a glimpse of shimmering sea, the Bristol Channel, down the line of the Clydach valley, before stopping at a dressed stone set upright at the edge of the path. This was inscribed with a large number 47 and the lettering *"The Gower Way"*. What on earth was the Gower Way doing up here at least thirty miles from that worthy peninsula? The explanation of this conundrum was that the Norman lordship of Gower originally extended well northwards of Swansea and included the terrain that I was now on.

Towards eleven-thirty I encountered another stone marker post for The Gower Way, number 46A, just before stepping onto the tarmac moorland road which ran north-south following the ridge. The map showed that I had exactly a kilometre of this ruler-straight road to cover before my planned turn-off into the forest by the Upper Lliw reservoir. It was dangerous going for the traffic hurtled down the long slope at breakneck speed and I realised that the objective of the motorists was to travel as fast as possible whilst completely ignoring the sunlit ridge and valley landscape. The Upper Lliw reservoir was visible as a glittering rhombus of water with a tower at its far end. The terrain was ridge and valley, rolling ridges brightly sunlit and verdant valleys to right and left, unnaturally green. I duly turned left off the road just beyond spot height 251 and entered the wood where a board informed me that:

"This is Bryn Llefrith plantation, planted between 1959 and 1961, and mostly coniferous trees, larch, Sitka spruce and Scots pine The trails and rides throughout the site provide excellent quiet walking routes suitable for all the family. Originally planted by the FC the woodland is now in the ownership of Hyder and is managed in partnership with the City and County of Swansea with support from the FC. The intention is slowly to convert the wood to a mixture of broadleaf and coniferous trees whilst providing a number of open spaces for picnics and

relaxation. These broadleaf species will be naturally regenerated from the trees that are already in the woodland..Today the plantation provides a wildlife habitat of wet areas on the western edge for a diverse and large population of damsel and dragonflies. There are a number of visiting pairs of red kites and peregrine falcons have also been recorded."

It was actually a fairly unpleasant piece of woodland to walk through. Its dark and dreary ambience was caused by the closely planted conifers, its generally unkempt and overgrown nature and its exceedingly wet ground. It was deserted, quiet and wild - still a bit of wild Wales. It was truly very quiet; there was no bird-song and indeed nothing to be heard save the tinkling of water in the trackside ditches.Further down toward the bottom of the wood the trees opened out to show a sun-dappled forest floor of mosses and grass. I had to climb a fence to leave the wood to follow the appalling muddy path which twisted and turned through gorse to the dam at the end of the reservoir. Here I paused to enjoy the vista of the placid water and the intricate but intimate valley which wound its way, bearing the Afon Lliw, through the hills southwards.

I intended to cross the last range of hills before the Swansea valley via Banc Maestir Mawr, 258 metres, which was evidently the last bastion of the hill country before the populated and industrial Swansea valley, and the M4. From the end of the reservoir I followed a vague path steeply uphill through some rough scrub, thorn and bracken. The multitude of paths shown on the map were not evident on the ground and, rather than stopping to get out my compass, I navigated by means of keeping a ruined house in line with the tower at the end of the reservoir, both of which did appear on the map and both of which I could see until I reached the summit at 258 metres. From there I had another sweeping view of Swansea and Gower, some in bright sunlight, some of it in dark cloud shadow, and a satanic glimpse through a gap in the hills of the smoke and steaming chimneys of the Port Talbot steelworks.

I paused for a while and viewed with dismay the ugly sprawl of the Swansea hinterland before me. What an abrupt and shocking contrast it made with the peaceful solitude of the terrain I was leaving.

Intending to reach the nearest public road, I spied a shining stack of black plastic silage bales, assumed that they must be at a farm and that it would be on a road and struck a bee-line across the flat and boggy hilltop in that direction. By sheer luck, or possibly some sub-conscious navigational skill, I hit the road at its end where the farm presented the usual ugly face of modern farming: the silage bales, huge grey corrugated barns, rusting machinery and, unusually, a sign which cryptically announced "RABBITS".

The lane followed the ridge-line and so still gave good views of the sea and the valley. Through typical, rather scruffy upland pasture I followed the lane southwards, squashing underfoot an unavoidable carpet of crab-apples, the abundance of which I'd never before seen. A makeshift sign by the road announced:
"Those who work with nature understand it.
Leave it to the experts or lose the rural life-line.
www.sockme. org".
Well, that was a bit too cryptic for me I'm afraid, accustomed though I am to completing the DT crossword. I realised that I'd seen no-one to speak to since the woman who was going to resume cycling. However, as I passed a very tidy pink cottage, I cried " HULLO, HOW ARE YOU?" to a man emptying a cement mixer but, as he totally ignored me, I decided not to pursue it.

Beyond Taironen I passed a large, but ugly, stone-built chapel in a congested burial ground where the headstones were unusually ornate, mostly of polished black marble with gold lettering, one or two Celtic crosses, urns on pillars and some older plain headstones in local stone whose legends had been eroded by the elements over the decades. It was the Salem

Baptist chapel, built in 1777, enlarged in 1815 and rebuilt in 1877 and what a heavy and opulent graveyard it had for an isolated country chapel. The footpath shortcut I'd intended to take shortly further on was not finger-posted from the road and the line of it seemed to be blocked by a pair of new bungalows and so I decided to avoid what would probably be aggravation (likely to be mostly canine) by sticking to the road. I turned left near the Swansea Waterworks so the city was evidently getting its water from the Upper Lliw reservoir. The M4 was less than three kilometres away but there was no sound of it; the countryside was still very peaceful and calm - grazing land but much acid upland vegetation of reeds, marsh grass and tussock.

I entered a very odd community at Aber Gelli Fach where the road suddenly widened to four times its normal width, where huge barn-type building crowded the road on one side and where a bulldozer was pushing mud around in a blasted, sodden patch of scrubby bog on the other. I couldn't make out whether it was agricultural or industrial, and there was no human activity to confirm either. At the end of this agglomeration, at a bend in the road, an ugly but neat house sat surrounded by immaculately maintained lawns where an old boy in a panama hat was driving an ancient red tractor pulling a gang-mower across the lawns that certainly had no need of further shaving. Round the bend the red theme was continued by the reddish tinge of that bog-loving grass that I had noted the day before on the wet descent from the Black Mountain, perhaps due to a surfeit of iron in the soil. Here the flat land to the right of the road was covered in a wild tangle of scrub but the grass beneath the bushes was the same peculiar shade of rusty-red. Perhaps there was a surfeit of iron in the local soil. The rather macabre atmosphere was accentuated by the two large orange balls that hung from the overhead electricity cables that crossed this bizarre plot of land.

At Llety Morfil I wanted to get off the road at last and follow the footpath towards Pant Lasau. But this was not easy, in the event, for an unsigned and vague path dodged around the perimeter of the garden of the house and then led to a patch of woodland where there was no gate or stile to cross the field fence. I climbed the fence with great difficulty only to find that a tracked machine had used the footpath down through the wood and turned it into a linear slurry pit that wasn't passable without wading through six inches of evil-smelling sludge. Which I had to do. Covered, by now, to the knees in mud, my temper wasn't improved by finding no gate or stile out of the wood and no waymarked route to Maes Eglwys. More fence climbing was needed to gain a field whose hedge I followed, to soon be blocked again by an unclimbable fence. More grovelling through thornscrub took me to a stream bed, or what I thought was a stream but which turned out to be the public right of way I was seeking.

This was evidently an old green lane which had become a watercourse. So from mud to water; at least my boots were getting a wash! This foul, streaming, overgrown and rubbish-strewn route led me eventually to drier ground and a lane near Maes Eglwys. To reach the lane I crossed a smart stile, freshly built with non-skid steps and waymarkers carefully screwed to the uprights. All rather pointless for, if you followed the markers, you'd be led to the brambly chaos at the edge of the wood and then the foul line of deep slurry in the trees. If you got that far. It seems to me that either you waymark the whole route from one road to another across country, or you don't waymark any of it. It's the inconsistency that's so irritating.

The farm lane led pleasantly through coppiced woodland to a stream crossing where the ford, still evident, had been superseded by a clumsy concrete bridge. Just at this point I could faintly hear, for the first time, the continual roar of the traffic on the motorway about a kilometre away. It was definitely not the stream or the wind in the trees but that distinctive incessant vehicle boom that only a motorway can produce. The lane continued pleasantly until, just before 2pm, I abruptly came to houses and the five-way road junction at Pant Lasau. Here the traffic was hectically speeding along the road to the hospital, creating a tumult which stunned me after the peace and quiet of the day's walk. I turned right to follow the ever-streaming traffic through scrubby farmland, overhead cables and electricity sub-stations - the urban hinterland of northern Swansea - towards the racketing motorway. This unpleasant walking continued as far as the roundabout at junction 46 where I bore left into quieter suburbia and arrived at the Plough and Harrow at Llangyfelach at nine minutes past two. That was as far as I was going. I'd begun the walk at the Black Boy Inn in Caernarfon and finished at another inn 262 kilometres distant.

So, that was it. Caernarfon to Swansea.. All under my own steam. No buses, taxis or trains. No driving. Just me and my two sore feet, rucksack, map and compass. I had travelled hopefully............ and I had arrived.

***

Meanings of some place names visited

Caernarfon	castle on the River Arfon
Castell Gidwm	wolf's castle
Tan y Bwlch	below the pass
Beddgelert	grave of Gelert
Pont yr Afon Gam	the bridge on the River Gam
Bwlch y Groes	the pass of the cross
Pen y Bont	the end of the bridge
Maesnant	place on the stream
Ysbyty Ystwyth	hospital on the River Ystwyth
Capel Gwynfa	chapel of paradise
Abertawe	mouth of the River Towy

Henryd

The Upper Lliw Reservoir

Brynamman

Journey's end at The Plough and Harrow, Llangyfelach

POSTSCRIPT

Had I enjoyed this walk?

Yes, indeed I had. From the initial reading of *Wild Wales*, to the careful plotting of the route that I should take to stay as close to Borrow's route as possible, to the execution of each day's walk and the heightened observation of the countryside that a meaningful account required, to the comparisons I drew between Borrow's observations and mine, I had taken great pleasure and satisfaction from the whole expedition.

I'd covered, under my own steam, some of the best remote lowland countryside that Wales could offer. I'd reached places that I would never otherwise have visited.

I'd had the opportunity to use my navigational skills with map, compass and intuition to follow a pre-determined line.

The natural geography hadn't changed since 1854 and the major change to the landscape had been caused by the infernal combustion engine and its need for tarmac roads. The towns and villages had grown by means of modern housing and industrial buildings.

The intrusive sounds that I heard: road vehicles, farm machinery, aircraft, quarry machinery and railway noise would not have been heard in 1854. Borrow's walk would have been a much more peaceful experience.

There had been a noticeable shift from rural to urban living in 150 years as shown by the number of derelict and ruined dwellings outside of the towns and by the general de-population of the countryside. Borrow had no difficulty meeting locals to talk to, indeed they seemed to pop up in the most unlikely places, whereas I could walk for miles and not see a soul.

There were now, as far as I could tell from listening and questioning those folk that I did meet, no Welsh who couldn't speak English (which there were in Borrow's time) and the speaking of Welsh as a first language now seemed confined to the remoter parts of N. Wales.

Borrow had to enquire about the names of villages, mountains, bridges, streams and rivers whereas I could cull these from the OS maps before reaching them. Although the Ordnance Survey was producing one inch maps of rural Wales in the 1850s, it is doubtful that these would have been widely available to travellers. Borrow makes no mention of maps in his book and so it's safe to assume that he had no maps on which to plot a route nor with which to orientate himself nor did he carry a compass all of which makes it more remarkable that he found his way to his destination each day and didn't get lost more often. Borrow had to ask his way around and it's just as well that there seemed to have been plenty of people about to ask.

He didn't have the use of the micro-cassette tape recorder which I used extensively but relied instead on paper and pencil. One can imagine the difficulty, or indeed impossibility, of recording long conversations by this method and some, as quoted in Wild Wales, were so long and complex that one has to query their accuracy.

Great estates had fallen into decay, grand mansions burnt to the ground or demolished, smallholdings expanded into agri-business and railways built where none had existed. Huge twentieth-century coniferous plantations now swathed acres of moorland. Vast quantities of goods can now be shipped with ease to remote towns and villages; whereas in 1854 this still mostly had to be done only by horse and cart and so communities had to be more self-sufficient.

Public rights of way did not exist in 1854 as they were not enshrined until the 1950s following the Access to The Countryside Act of 1949. Thus Borrow, even if he'd had maps, wouldn't have know where, off-road, he could legally walk without let or hindrance. Our public rights of way system is a remarkable boon for walkers and riders and is largely unknown outside the UK.

There was no domestic electricity available in 1854 so Borrow would have seen no pylons marching across the terrain; no poles by the roadside and no street lamps. Indoor lighting after dark was created by candles and spirit lamps.

Telephones didn't exist either until Bell's invention of 1877. So there were no telephone poles in lines across the countryside. Borrow would not have been able to phone ahead to book accommodation and he certainly couldn't have made an instant call if he was injured in remote terrain, as we can do now.

Nearly everthing that George Borrow saw, I also saw, but much of what I saw, in terms of the infrastructure of our twenty-first century, he didn't see because it wasn't there.

Our respective appreciations and descriptions of the countryside, its buildings and its people were very different, separated by 150 years of culture change and as viewed by two very different men with dis-similar backgrounds and life experiences.

In view of the low-tec world that Borrow inhabited, the pilgimage was, for him, a more arduous and dangerous undertaking than mine.

I take my hat off to him - I really do.

***

The first edition of George Borrow's book 'Wild Wales' was published in 1862. My edition was published by Collins as a reprint in 1965 with an introduction by Cecil Price. It is a cloth-bound hardback with very flimsy pages. However, it survived twelve long days in my rucksack which is a testimonial to the durability of the binding. It is now just starting to come apart, to my dismay.

BV - #0081 - 300425 - C12 - 229/152/9 - PB - 9781914002595 - Gloss Lamination